FINDING FAVOR

with

GOD

#1 *NEW YORK TIMES* BESTSELLING AUTHOR

MIKE EVANS

TIMEWORTHY
BOOKS

P.O. BOX 30000, PHOENIX, AZ 85046

To my beloved wife, Carolyn Sue,
mother of our four precious children
and ten cherished grandchildren:
You and I were best friends before we fell in love.
You were the first person to ever believe in me,
and I am thankful that you still do.
You are my partner in ministry and
the most selfless person I've ever known.

INTRODUCTION

IN 2012, I RELATED some of my personal experiences in a book titled *Living in the FOG (Favor of God)*. It detailed how we, as Believers, could have God's favor at work in our lives. More recently, the question in the forefront of my thoughts has been: What is favor *with* God, and does that differ from the favor *of* God? That may best be explained by an example from my own life.

Also in 2012, I traveled to Jerusalem to seek a location for a Friends of Zion (FOZ) Museum in the Holy City. Through the museum, the accounts of Christians who played a crucial role in helping to promote, defend, support, and establish the modern state of Israel will be told, as will the stories of those men and women who fulfilled their moral duty to rescue Jewish people from the Holocaust. The attractive building that houses the museum sits in the heart of Jerusalem at 20 and 22 Yosef Rivlin Street, a prominent location overlooking Independence Park and within walking distance to the Old City.

My heart is overflowing with gratitude to God as the fulfillment of a dream He placed in my spirit more than thirty years ago has become a reality. When the contract for the purchase of the building that now houses FOZ—just a short distance from the Temple Mount—was signed, I was reminded once again that every promise from God is certain and sure, no matter how long we have to wait for it. Not only has this "great and effective door...opened to me (1 Corinthians 16:9)," God has made it possible for us to purchase an adjacent building to use as a welcome center and coffee shop.

Abraham waited for the promised birth of Isaac for some twenty-five years, but in God's perfect timing, the son of promise was born. Likewise, when I first met with Prime Minister Menachem Begin more than thirty years ago and we agreed to work together to build a bridge between Christians and Jews, part of that dream was to have a permanent presence in the Holy City. Now we are moving forward with this beautiful facility to minister to the Jewish people and to you.

Prior to that meeting with the prime minister, I had faced one of the greatest crises of my life: I was working eighteen hours a day, seven days a week, striving to be the best I could be, but not totally relying on God for His direction. I was soon beset with a neurological disease that manifested itself in neck spasms. At the same time, I began to experience panic attacks and tachycardia (a sudden increase in heart rate). In the midst of this darkness, I became depressed, discouraged, and physically drained. I cried out to God from the midst of a cardiology ward, "Lord, what am I doing wrong? I need Your peace." As I said that, the Lord whispered in my spirit, *"Then you shall know Me in the power of My resurrection."* Little did I know that several months later, the soft, gentle voice of the Holy Spirit would urge me to read:

> Remember ye not the former things, neither con-
> sider the things of old. Behold, I will do a new thing;
> now it shall spring forth; shall ye not know it? I will

even make a way in the wilderness, and rivers in the desert (Isaiah 43:18–19 KJV).

Through this Scripture it was as though a drop of water had fallen on my parched spirit. Next the Holy Spirit instructed me to go home and send a fax to Israeli Prime Minister Begin, asking if he would meet with me. I was reluctant to reach out to a man who did not know me. Eventually, I obeyed the voice of God and sent the fax telling the prime minister I would be in a Jerusalem hotel for six days and expressing my desire to meet with him. I flew there, checked in to my hotel, and began to pray.

On the second day, I found myself surrounded by the favor of God as I answered a call to meet with the prime minister. Mr. Begin dominated the conversation for almost thirty minutes, which was a relief because I could think of nothing to say.

Finally he asked, "Why did you come?"

"I don't know why I came," I answered.

"You don't know?" he said with astonishment. "What *do* you know?"

"God sent me," I said.

"God sent you but didn't tell you why?" he asked, becoming amused at the situation.

"No, He didn't tell me why," I said, somewhat embarrassed.

He called for his secretary to come into his office.

"Eight thousand miles, Kadashai, to meet with me, and he says nothing except God sent him. Kadashai, shake his hand. We have finally found an honest man!"

Then he turned to me and said, "When God tells you why, will you come back and tell me?"

After leaving the prime minister's office I still didn't know why

I'd come, so I prayed and waited for an answer. Finally Jesus softly spoke one word to me: *"Bridge."* Once I had that, I called and we set another time to meet.

When we met, the prime minister asked, "Why did you come?"

I replied slowly, "To build a bridge."

"What kind of bridge? The Brooklyn Bridge?" the prime minister chuckled.

"A bridge of love...between Christians in America and Jews in Israel," I answered.

"I like that," Begin said. "Let's build it together."

Before I left his office, the prime minister gave me two letters he had written and asked me to deliver them. One was addressed to Dr. Billy Graham and the other to Dr. Jerry Falwell. I had told him earlier that I knew neither man. He assured me these letters would open doors for me.

That was the start of more than three decades of a Jesus-blessed ministry to the nation of Israel. It revolutionized my life and helped develop the bridge Jesus wanted built.

By my not caring about my reputation, God was able to use me. Somehow I fit into His plan, allowing my imperfections to draw me closer to Him.

That bridge has been built because over the years I have been blessed not only with the favor *of* God, but I have walked in favor *with* God. The favor *of* God has opened doors for me; favor *with* God has given me the grace and strength to walk through those doors to experience the full blessings of God in my life and ministry.

CHAPTER ONE

GOD'S POWER AND PRESENCE

The heavens declare the glory of God;
And the firmament shows His handiwork.

—PSALM 19:1

IN 1978 THE LATE Jamie Buckingham, international author and columnist, invited me to accompany his group on what had become for him a regular trek through the Sinai. It would be an unforgettable journey through the desert—one filled with sand, sun, scorching heat, scorpions, and a stunning example of God's presence. Lying on my back on the hard, rocky ground one night, my eyes were filled with the wonder of creation. I understood firsthand how David must have felt as he watched over his father's sheep in the hills of Judea.

It must have been there that he sang the first words of Psalm 19. Perhaps he, like me, was lying on his back staring in awe at God's handiwork, so much more visible in the darkness of the desert. But it is often in the night hours, in the rocky places, that God reveals His power and presence to His children. His skill and artistry is then on full display in the heavens.

It was on a cold, dark night outside Bethlehem that He announced the birth of a baby. It was not written on parchment, but heralded by a host of angels who lit up the dark sky and gladdened the hearts of a lonely group of shepherds with their song. It was a personal invitation to come and see the Christ child, the Messiah, the Savior of all mankind. It was proof yet again that while the Creator hung the stars and planets, the sun and moon in the skies above, His message was and is still carried by men and women.

In October 1982, a member of my ministry team and I were on our way home in a private plane piloted by a friend. We had just completed taping a television special, *Israel: America's Key to Survival*. As we neared our destination, one of the engines of the plane malfunctioned, and we could smell smoke and fuel; the lights on the instrument panel had gone out, and we were flying blind in a dark sky. As I rebuked the Destroyer, my team member began to pray, "Angels of the Lord, undergird us...angels of the Lord, undergird us."

Twenty-one minutes later we landed near Fort Worth. When the pilot looked over the plane, we were astonished to learn that one engine had broken loose and was totally drained of oil. We had truly experienced the power and presence of God on that flight—a miracle. The following morning, a ministry partner, Mrs. Obel, called the office and reported to my secretary that the previous night she had been awakened from sleep and impressed to pray that the Lord would undergird me wherever I was. All she could pray for thirty minutes was, "Angels of the Lord, undergird Mike; angels of the Lord, undergird Mike." What Satan meant for evil on that dark and starless night, God turned to good.

Just as David reveled in the awe of God's power and presence in the night sky, so did the apostle Peter see a miraculous expression of God's power and presence in the darkness of a storm. It has been said that it is impossible for a Believer to face the future unless strengthened by a powerful and loving God. Peter learned that lesson well on the stormy Sea of Galilee.

Matthew 14:22–34 teaches a lesson on the authority of our Lord over creation. Jesus had spent a long and physically draining day of exhorting, instructing, and healing a vast assembly of people that had followed Him to a deserted beach. He had fed soul and spirit with His words. He then fed the hungry multitude of five thousand men, plus an unspecified number of women and children, with a meal miraculously produced from five loaves and two fish. In His humanity, He must have surely been exhausted.

As night slowly descended over the Sea of Galilee, He sent His disciples across to the other side. Matthew 14:23–24 says, "And when He had sent the multitudes away, He went up on the mountain by Himself to pray. Now when evening came, He was alone there. But the boat was now in the middle of the sea, tossed by the waves, for the wind was contrary."

Matthew tells us it was the "fourth watch of the night." According to one commentary:

> The Jews at this time divided the night into four watches; the first was from six o'clock in the evening till nine, the second from nine to twelve, the third from twelve till three, and the fourth from three till six.[1]

In His agony of prayer, Jesus heard the distant cries of His disciples who were battling the storm. Rising from the ground, the Son of Man laid aside His exhaustion and assumed His role as Lord and Master of the waves. He strode down to the water's edge, stepped onto the stormy sea as if it were dry ground, and walked out toward the wallowing craft. The disciples, spotting the apparition coming toward the boat, cried out in fear, "It's a ghost!" Matthew takes up the story here in verses 27–33:

> But immediately Jesus spoke to them, saying, "Be of good cheer! It is I; do not be afraid." And Peter answered Him and said, "Lord, if it is You, command me to come to You on the water." So He said, "Come." And when Peter had come down out of the boat, he walked on the water to go to Jesus. But when he saw that the wind was boisterous, he was afraid; and beginning to sink he cried out, saying, "Lord, save me!" And immediately Jesus stretched out His hand and caught him, and said to him, "O you of little faith, why did you doubt?" And when they got into the boat, the wind ceased. Then those who were in the boat came and worshiped Him, saying, "Truly You are the Son of God."

Immediately, the disciples realized that their fears were unjustified when compared to the power and presence of Jesus. Believers today must grasp the same understanding: Jesus has not forsaken His children in the midst of the storm; He is ever present, ever powerful, and loves us unconditionally. The popular poem, "Footprints in the Sand", ends with these reassuring words:

> I have noticed that during the most troublesome
>   times in my life,
> There is only one set of footprints.

I don't understand why in times when I needed you
    the most, you should leave me.
The Lord replied, "My precious, precious child.
I love you, and I would never, never leave you during
    your times of trial and suffering.
When you saw only one set of footprints,
It was then that I carried you.[2]

Deuteronomy 31:6 reminds us, "Be strong and of good courage, do not fear nor be afraid of them; for the LORD your God, He *is* the One who goes with you. He will not leave you nor forsake you." In the darkest nights, even when you can't see Him, He is there and is watching over you. As Lauryn Hill sang in her version of the beautiful song "His Eye Is on the Sparrow":

I sing because I'm happy,
I sing because I'm free,
His eye is on the sparrow,
And I know He watches me.[3]

Even during those times when we don't know how to pray or even what to pray, we have the assurance in Romans 8:26–27 that the Holy Spirit is interceding for us:

For we do not know what we should pray for as we ought, but the Spirit Himself makes intercession for us with groanings which cannot be uttered. Now He who searches the hearts knows what the mind of the Spirit is, because He makes intercession for the saints according to the will of God.

Fear no longer has to rule the life of a Believer. That was another lesson well learned when I found myself in the emergency room shrouded by drapes and awaiting a diagnosis for what I feared was a heart attack. The curtains were closed around my bed, and I felt certain someone had died. I thought, *Oh, lovely! I guess I'm next.*

The ER doctor ordered a stress test and advised me, "If the red light comes on, it means you are having a heart attack." When the red light flashed brightly, the newly graduated technician administering the test ran from the room in a panic. There I was on the treadmill, alone, certain I was having a heart attack. On the verge of a panic attack, I finally freed myself from the machine and sank into a chair. As I sat there trying to slow my beating heart, the technician returned and apologized. "Sorry, Mr. Evans, it was the electrical system. It shorted out."

I replied with what little humor I could muster, "Now I know why it's called a stress test." With the test completed, I was admitted to a room to await the results. There I was, flat on my back and greatly in need of someone in whom I could confide—but whom? A name popped into my mind and I reached for the telephone. In a few minutes I was connected to the one person I felt I could trust: my good friend Jamie Buckingham.

Not only did this busy man answer the phone when it rang, he took time for me. My voice cracked as I said, "Jamie, this is Mike Evans. I'm in the hospital cardiology ward." A sob tore from my throat, "I'm scared, Jamie." Jamie and I talked for a bit, and he assured me that God was more than able to handle my fears and give me His peace in the midst of the storm. As I hung up the phone, I knew there was Someone else I needed to spend time with—my Lord. I lifted my hands heavenward in surrender and began to confess my fears to the God of all peace.

The official diagnosis was tachycardia. My work habits were partly to blame. I simply had failed to take care of this body God has given me. Fortunately, I hadn't had a heart attack, but the doctor warned that I might very well find myself in that place if I didn't change my ways.

As you and I seek to move into a closer relationship with Jesus through prayer and Bible study, attitudes begin to change, faith flourishes, and the result is total assurance in our Lord. We find comfort in His power and presence. We receive boldness that we can endure whatever lies in our pathway because of Jesus, King of kings, Lord of lords, our omnipotent, omniscient, loving Savior and Redeemer! With Jesus as our Champion, no foe can stand against us!

Knowing that, we grow more positive that God will make provision for us. Our Lord is the victor in every situation. In Romans, chapter 8, the apostle Paul states emphatically that nothing can remove us from His hand:

> What then shall we say to these things? If God is for us, who can be against us? He who did not spare His own Son, but delivered Him up for us all, how shall He not with Him also freely give us all things? ...Who shall separate us from the love of Christ? Shall tribulation, or distress, or persecution, or famine, or nakedness, or peril, or sword? ... Yet in all these things we are more than conquerors through Him who loved us. For I am persuaded that neither death nor life, nor angels nor principalities nor powers, nor things present nor things to come, nor height nor depth, nor any other created thing, shall be able to

separate us from the love of God which is in Christ Jesus our Lord (vv. 31–32, 35, 37–39).

What a wonderful promise to the Believer! Nothing—no thing—can separate us from God's power and presence, from His love and grace. Many of the books in the New Testament contain the phrase "grace to you" or "grace be with you." It was not added as just a congenial greeting. Paul, who wrote many of the epistles, and the other writers who used that particular salutation were well aware of the necessity of God's grace or favor.

The power and presence of God was so unmistakable in the life of Abraham that even unbelievers could see the difference in his life. In Genesis 20 and 21, we read of the relationship between the Philistine King Abimelech and Abraham and the covenant that was established between the two men. Although their earlier encounter had been less than positive, it soon became evident to the king that God was with Abraham in everything he did (see Genesis 21:22). His herds were increasing; the number of servants was growing; Abraham was blessed by the power and presence of God in his life. As a result, Abimelech feared the potential for conflict with this man who found favor with God. This heathen king realized that God blessed, guided, and protected Abraham and that wherever he went the power and presence of God covered him.

Judges 6 relates the story of Gideon, a man who was basically a wimp! When we first meet Gideon in this chapter, he is hiding in fear from the Midianites in order to thresh wheat for his family. And yet when the angel of the Lord approached Gideon, his greeting in verse 12 was, "The LORD is with you, you mighty man of valor!" Can you imagine what Gideon's response might have been? "Who me? Mighty?" In fact, that could be a modern translation of what he did say in verse 15:

> O my Lord, how can I save Israel? Indeed my clan is the weakest in Manasseh, and I am the least in my father's house.

Not a very courageous beginning for a deliverer. In his own eyes, Gideon was a zero, a nobody, a failure, and certainly not a "mighty man of valor," as he had been addressed. He was pretty sure God could not use him for anything, much less something that required boldness! He viewed his life as one without the power and presence of Jehovah God. Apparently he had not heard the totality of what the angel had said in verse 14:

> Go in this might of yours, and you shall save Israel from the hand of the Midianites. Have I not sent you?

In essence, God was saying to Gideon: "You don't know what you can do when you allow yourself to be accompanied by My presence and filled with My power." He was making the same promise to Gideon that He had made to Moses in Exodus 33:14, "My Presence will go with you, and I will give you rest."

Gideon was slow to warm up to the idea of being a mighty man of valor, to be the one chosen of God to engage the entire Midianite army in battle. He could not comprehend that God wanted *him* for the task at hand. He was not some superhero, but he had two things in his favor: God's power and presence.

Hudson Taylor, the great pioneer missionary to China, might

well have described Gideon's life when he said, "I have found that there are three stages in every great work of God: first, it is impossible, then it is difficult, then it is done."[4]

Despite God's assurance that he was the man for the job, Gideon finally chose to obey God—but not during the daylight hours; it was in the middle of the night. He quietly issued a call for the people to gather and was astounded when 32,000 showed up! But God had a different plan, one that would further challenge Gideon's dependence on Him. Imagine his dismay when God told Gideon the army was too large and introduced His plan to streamline the troops to a mere 10,000 men. Even then, God determined that number to be too large and devised one further test:

> "Everyone who laps from the water with his tongue, as a dog laps, you shall set apart by himself; likewise everyone who gets down on his knees to drink." And the number of those who lapped, putting their hand to their mouth, was three hundred men; but all the rest of the people got down on their knees to drink water. Then the Lord said to Gideon, "By the three hundred men who lapped I will save you, and deliver the Midianites into your hand" (Judges 7:5–7).

Three hundred men! That was Gideon's army. The Midianite army was said to be "without number" (see Judges 7:12). Yet Gideon obeyed God's very specific instructions. Each man was to carry a trumpet and a pitcher with a torch inside. The men were divided into three companies of one hundred each and spread around the perimeter of the Midianite camp. At the appointed time, they were to blow their trumpets, smash the lamps, and yell, "The sword of the LORD and of Gideon" (Judges 7:20b).

When the cacophony of noise awoke the Midianites, they were seized with panic and fled before the army of the Lord. Gideon pursued the enemy until it was vanquished:

> Thus Midian was subdued before the children of Israel, so that they lifted their heads no more. And the country was quiet for forty years in the days of Gideon (Judges 8:28).

Gideon could have walked away from God's plan at any time. In the natural, it must have seemed totally impossible to win Israel's freedom from the marauding, murderous Midianites. However, Gideon chose to believe that the power and presence of Jehovah-Mephalti—the Lord my Deliverer—was greater than the multitude of Midianite militia.

Jeremiah was a prophet ordained by God to deliver a message of judgment to Israel, an unappreciated job at best. Unfortunately, his message was not designed to win friends; he was to simply speak only "Thus says the LORD" (see Jeremiah 15:2). Jeremiah did exactly that; he pronounced judgment and destruction on Israel because of their sins. He warned, "I [Jehovah] will cause anguish and terror to fall on them suddenly" (see verse 8).

But Jeremiah's message was not totally one of devastation, for God always provides a way of escape for His people, a glimmer of hope in a dark world. He promised, "If you return, Then I will bring you back; You shall stand before Me (see verse 19).

The reaction to Jeremiah's message was to be expected; the people were incensed. Plans were made to cast him in prison without possibility of a reprieve. The prophet reacted much as you or I might have: He vowed to stop preaching and began to complain. He whined in prayer:

> Then Jeremiah replied, "Lord, you know it is for your sake that I am suffering. They are persecuting me because I have proclaimed your word to them. Don't let them kill me! Rescue me from their clutches, and give them what they deserve! Your words are what sustain me; they are food to my hungry soul. They bring joy to my sorrowing heart and delight me. How proud I am to bear your name, O Lord. I have not joined the people in their merry feasts. I sit alone beneath the hand of God. I burst with indignation at their sins. Yet you have failed me in my time of need! You have let them keep right on with all their persecutions. Will they never stop hurting me? Your help is as uncertain as a seasonal mountain brook—sometimes a flood, sometimes as dry as a bone" (Jeremiah 15:15–18 TLB).

Jeremiah reacted much like Elijah did in 1 Kings 19:4, 9–10:

> But he himself went a day's journey into the wilderness, and came and sat down under a broom tree. And he prayed that he might die, and said, "It is enough! Now, LORD, take my life, for I am no better than my fathers!" And there [at Mount Horeb] he went into a cave, and spent the night in that place; and behold, the word of the LORD came to him, and

He said to him, "What are you doing here, Elijah?" So he said, "I have been very zealous for the LORD God of hosts; for the children of Israel have forsaken Your covenant, torn down Your altars, and killed Your prophets with the sword. I alone am left; and they seek to take my life."

Both prophets had basically the same thoughts: *Okay, Lord, I did what you told me to do and you have abandoned me.* At that moment, Jeremiah must have felt forsaken and alone.

Then in verses 19–21, God made the promise of His power and presence to His spokesman:

"If you return, then I will bring you back; you shall stand before Me; if you take out the precious from the vile, you shall be as My mouth. Let them return to you, but you must not return to them. And I will make you to this people a fortified bronze wall; and they will fight against you, but they shall not prevail against you; for I am with you to save you and deliver you," says the LORD. "I will deliver you from the hand of the wicked, and I will redeem you from the grip of the terrible."

God was calling Jeremiah to stop complaining and bellyaching, to cease his incessant grumbling! But He doesn't stop there; He reminds Jeremiah of the promises He made to him when he was first called to preach Jehovah's message. He is promised the power of God, the security of the Holy One of Israel to defend against those who threaten him. God reminded Jeremiah that it didn't matter what the people thought of him, only what God had promised—His power and presence to accompany the prophet.

It's reminiscent of another prophet to whom God gave a promise:

> Fear not, for I have redeemed you; I have called you by your name; you are Mine. When you pass through the waters, I will be with you; and through the rivers, they shall not overflow you. When you walk through the fire, you shall not be burned, nor shall the flame scorch you (Isaiah 43:1–2).

Favor with God can accomplish what your greatest talents and abilities cannot—unlocking doors you may think are locked, eliminating hurdles hindering your advancement, presenting unexpected openings, and bidding you to enter elite alliances and develop new associations. In today's job market terms, favor allows you access to God's network. Seek favor with God; stand before Him in sincerity and submission; offer His grace and favor to others; enjoy favor with God. 2 Corinthians 6:2 (niv), bids us to come and partake, *"Now is the time of God's favor, now is the day of salvation."*

— DISCUSSION —
MATERIAL

1. Read Matthew 14:23–33.

2. The disciples felt alone on the sea at night. Why do you think trials and troubles seem so much more difficult in the night hours?

3. What should we do at those times?

4. God called Gideon to deliver the Israelites. Why do you think God chose a fearful young man to lead His people?

5. Has God called you to do something for which you feel unqualified?

6. Like Jeremiah, have you ever been asked to deliver a message that may not have been well-received?

7. What was your response?

8. What was the outcome?

9. Has there been a time in your life when you particularly felt God's power and presence surround you?

—SCRIPTURES ON—
GOD'S POWER AND PRESENCE

Honor and majesty are [found] in His presence; strength
and joy are [found] in His sanctuary.
1 CHRONICLES 16:27 AMP

And he said, "My presence will go with you, and I will give
you rest."
EXODUS 33:14 ESV

You will show me the path of life; in Your presence
is fullness of joy; at Your right hand are pleasures
forevermore.
PSALM 16:11

You shall hide them in the secret place of Your presence
from the plots of man; You shall keep them secretly in a
pavilion from the strife of tongues.
PSALM 31:20

Do not cast me away from Your presence and do not
take Your Holy Spirit from me.
PSALM 51:11 NASB

Be silent in the presence of the Lord GOD; for the day of the
LORD is at hand, for the LORD has prepared a sacrifice; He
has invited His guests.
ZEPHANIAH 1:7

Repent therefore and be converted, that your sins may be
blotted out, so that times of refreshing may come from the
presence of the Lord.
ACTS 3:19

Where can I go from Your Spirit?
Or where can I flee from Your presence?
PSALM 139:7

Serve the LORD with gladness: come before his presence
with singing.
PSALM 100:2 KJV

The mountains melt like wax at the presence of the LORD,
at the presence of the Lord of the whole earth.
PSALM 97:5

Now to Him who is able to keep you from stumbling,
and to present you faultless before the presence of His glory
with exceeding joy, to God our Savior, who alone is wise,
be glory and majesty, dominion and power, both now and
forever. Amen.
JUDE 1:24–25

When my enemies turn back, they shall fall and perish at
Your presence.
PSALM 9:3

The earth shook; the heavens also dropped rain at the
presence of God; Sinai itself was moved at the presence of
God, the God of Israel.
PSALM 68:8

Let us come before His presence with thanksgiving; let us
shout joyfully to Him with psalms.
PSALM 95:2

Tremble, O earth, at the presence of the Lord, at the
presence of the God of Jacob.
PSALM 114:7

Surely the righteous shall give thanks to Your name; the
upright shall dwell in Your presence.
PSALM 140:13

For Christ did not send me to baptize but to preach the
gospel, and not with words of eloquent wisdom, lest the
cross of Christ be emptied of its power. For the word of the

cross is folly to those who are perishing, but to us who are being saved it is the power of God.
1 CORINTHIANS 1:17–18 ESV

Finally, be strong in the Lord and in the power of his might. Put on the whole armor of God, that you may be able to stand against the schemes of the devil. For we do not wrestle against flesh and blood, but against the rulers, against the authorities, against the cosmic powers over this present darkness, against the spiritual forces of evil in the heavenly places. Therefore take up the whole armor of God, that you may be able to withstand in the evil day, and having done all, to stand firm. Stand therefore, having fastened on the belt of truth, and having put on the breastplate of righteousness, and, as shoes for your feet, having put on the readiness given by the gospel of peace. In all circumstances take up the shield of faith, with which you can extinguish all the flaming darts of the evil one; and take the helmet of salvation, and the sword of the Spirit, which is the word of God, praying at all times in the Spirit, with all prayer and supplication. To that end keep alert with all perseverance, making supplication for all the saints...
EPHESIANS 6:10–18 ESV

Indeed, I count everything as loss because of the surpassing worth of knowing Christ Jesus my Lord. For his sake I have suffered the loss of all things and count them as rubbish, in order that I may gain Christ and be found in him, not having a righteousness of my own that comes from the law, but that which comes through faith in Christ, the righteousness from God that depends on faith—that I may know him and the power of his resurrection, and may share his sufferings, becoming like him in his death, that by any means possible I may attain the resurrection from the dead.
PHILIPPIANS 3:8–11 ESV

CHAPTER TWO

GOD'S PROTECTION

*"You shall not be afraid of the terror by night,
nor of the arrow that flies by day..."*

PSALM 91:5

IN 1983, I TRAVELED TO LEBANON to deliver food, medicine, and Bibles to the people there. Minutes before reaching the city of Sidon, the PLO bombed the area. Had our arrival been any earlier, we could well have been caught in the crossfire. We distributed supplies and then headed for Beirut. We met with US marines on a beachhead by the Mediterranean Sea, ministering to them, giving them Bibles, and praying with them.

Later that evening the troops returned to their barracks at Beirut International Airport, approximately 500 yards from the beachhead. Our team unrolled our sleeping bags and made our beds on the sandy beach. A little after 6:00 a.m. the following morning I was standing on the beachhead talking to a contingent of marines who had just taken up their posts. Suddenly a terrific explosion rent the air.

We would soon learn that as the American troops were beginning a new day, the marine sentry at the gate looked up to see a big yellow Mercedes truck barreling down. The sentry reported that the driver of the truck smiled at him as he crashed through the gates. The truck was on a course for the lobby of the barracks. The sentries, armed only with loaded pistols, were unable to stop the speeding vehicle.

The truck carried explosives equal to about six tons of TNT. The driver rammed into the lower floor of the barracks and discharged his deadly cargo. The explosion was so great that the four-story building collapsed in a heap of rubble. Many of the dead had not been killed by the blast itself, but were crushed beneath the cinder-block building as it pancaked in on itself.

News would soon spread that Islamic Jihad, a pseudonym for Iranian armed and funded Hezbollah terrorists, had taken credit for the attack that had blown up the marine barracks. The explosion and collapse of the building killed 241 American servicemen: 220 marines, eighteen navy personnel, and three army soldiers. Huge guns from warships off the coast of Beirut began to shell the area in retaliation.

Approximately two minutes following the blast at the marine barracks, terrorists attacked French troops stationed at Drakkar building in Beirut. The First Parachute Chasseur Regiment lost fifty-eight paratroopers with fifteen wounded. It was the most deadly loss for the French military since the Algerian War (1954–1962). It was my introduction to how vile and deadly terror attacks can be.

Upon hearing the explosion, my friends and I hurriedly gathered our belongings and headed for Nahariya, Israel, on the border. I had followed the sea to Beirut, but it would be dark soon. That became a problem as we drove south. I made several wrong turns that took us to Tyre and into the midst of the funeral procession of a Hezbollah operative. Our vehicle was an Avis rental car from Jerusalem with a distinctive Israeli license plate—not a good thing to have when you're surrounded by raging, grieving terrorists. Somehow God blinded their eyes and we were able to get through the city.

Once we reached the outskirts, I made another wrong turn. Instead of going to Nahariya, we were headed down a dirt road toward Damascus. Soon our vehicle was spotlighted and tracer bullets raced overhead, then 37-millimeter mortars began to crash into the desert near us.

We had been on God's business, and now we were being targeted! Next, our car's engine sputtered and died. We had left Beirut so quickly I had forgotten to check the fuel tank. Now we were lost on a desert road, amid hostile fighters, and out of fuel. What else could happen? There seemed no way to survive. It could only be a matter of minutes before our vehicle would be blown to shreds.

One of the men with me shouted, "We're dead!"

"You're not dead; you're talking! We have to pray," I responded. As I began to petition heaven for our safety, I was startled by a rap on the car window. Despite my bravado, I jumped at the sound. I thought, *This is it! We're going to meet our Maker on the backside of nowhere. God help us!* Standing there was a young Arab wearing a *kaffiyeh*—the traditional head covering—and hefting not a weapon but a fuel can. I wondered how he could possibly have known we were out of diesel.

He went to the back of the car, removed the fuel cap, and poured the diesel into the tank. He then walked over to the passenger door and pointed at the lock. I hesitated only briefly before pulling up the lock. He opened the door and climbed inside.

"Drive," he ordered. We had no idea where he was taking us.

I looked in the rearview mirror at my passengers, shrugged, and complied. For thirty-two kilometers the young man did not speak another word, only pointed in the direction he wished the car to go. After what seemed like hours, he barked, "Stop." The man opened the door and climbed from the car. He stuck his head back inside, said, "Safe," and then slammed the door.

I turned to look at my friends in the backseat—when I turned back, the young man was gone. We were out in the open. There was no place for him to disappear as quickly as he had. No one spoke a word until we drove over the border into Israel. One of my friends looked at me in awe and asked, "Can you explain what just happened?" I couldn't, other than that God answered the prayers for safety that had been prayed over us before we left Beirut.

Psalm 91 is a wonderful song of God's precious protection over His people. As the Believer reads through the chapter, it is soon evident that God doesn't promise that we will never find ourselves in tight places, in desperate situations, or be exempt from trouble or affliction. It does promise that God will walk with us through each trial and tribulation. He is omnipresent—everywhere—and is our Strong Deliverer, our Mighty Tower, our Strong Refuge, our ever-present help in time of need. God has promised never to leave us alone.

Each time God provides a way of escape for His children, it is a time for rejoicing and confidence-building. Favor with God is the path of protection. No matter the situation or circumstance, our heavenly Father is there to walk through it with us. The Believer is never alone.

The story is told of an early American Indian tribe with a unique method of transitioning their youngsters from childhood to Brave. After thirteen years of training in every aspect of becoming a warrior—hunting, scouting, riding, and survival in the wilderness—the young man would spend an entire night alone in the forest, away from the scrutiny and security of his tribal family. On the night in question, he would be blindfolded and led deep into the dark woods several miles from the village.

When he removed the blindfold, he found himself alone in the black night, surrounded by strange sounds. Each time a twig snapped, he imagined a dangerous animal stalking him. After what seemed like an eternity in a sleepless night, the first rays of sunlight penetrated the forest. Looking around, the boy spotted the path that would lead him to safety. As he started forward, he was utterly amazed to find his father, armed with a bow and arrow, sitting near a tree a few feet away. The father had been keeping watch all night long.[5]

The pages of Scripture are rife with descriptions of God's divine protection. The list is long and the stories amazing: Daniel was lion food; the three Hebrew men were fire fodder; Moses was cargo in a reed boat; David was a giant's bull's-eye; Elijah was a king's nemesis; and the list goes on and on. In each instance, God provided supernatural protection; He safeguarded His children.

Let's look again at Psalm 91:1–2:

> He who dwells in the secret place of the Most High
> shall abide under the shadow of the Almighty. I will
> say of the LORD, "He is my refuge and my fortress;
> My God, in Him I will trust."

Like the psalmist, the Believer has a choice to make: Dwell in the "secret place" or walk in the counsel of the ungodly and stand in the path of sinners.[6] The place of Psalm 91 is a place of safety and protection, a place where we are totally dependent on God. It is a place of strength for the obedient; the only true sanctuary. All the blessings of God are available to the one who "abides under the shadow of the Almighty."

In the *Treasury of David* commentary, writer Charles Spurgeon explains what is meant by God's protection:

> Abiding denotes a constant and continuous dwelling of the just in the assistance and protection of God. That help and protection of God is not like a lodge in a garden of cucumbers, or in a vineyard; which is destroyed in a moment, nor is it like a tent in the way which is abandoned by the traveler. It is a strong tower, a paternal home, wherein we spend all our life with the best, wealthiest, and mightiest of parents. Passing the night also denotes security and rest in time of darkness, temptations and calamities.[7]

God's protection is not some nebulous, abstract thing; it is a demonstrable element. God's Word declares that we are surrounded, embraced, sheltered, and overtaken by His kindness and are secure in Him. How all-encompassing is God's love for us and protection over us! Another thing you have to do to ensure God's protection besides walking with God and obeying Him is to speak your faith. The psalmist declares, "I will say of the Lord, '*He is* my refuge and my fortress'" (v. 2, emphasis added).

The psalmist gives us a mighty tool in invoking the Lord's protection in Psalm 91:2: "I will say of the LORD …" He reminds us that we must speak up. The tongue is a powerful force, either for good or evil. When we speak the Word in faith, it is a powerful reminder of God's grace and favor in our lives. When faced with the tempta-tions of the Enemy in the wilderness, Jesus did not just "think" his responses. No, He spoke out against the wiles of Satan. His physical weakness from the lack of food did not deter His faith in the Father. He declared the Word with power and conviction, and as a result received the benefits of God's protection.

Missionaries Matt and Lora Higgens tell the story of God's protection in Kenya during the Mau Mau uprising. The two were returning to Nairobi one night when:

> Seventeen miles outside of Nairobi their Land Rover stopped. Higgens tried to repair the car in the dark, but could not restart it. They spent the night in the car, but claimed Psalm 4:8: "I will lie down and sleep in peace, for you alone, O Lord, make me dwell in safety." In the morning they were able to repair the car. A few weeks later the Higgenses returned to America on furlough. They reported that the night before they left Nairobi, a local pastor had visited them [in his home]. He told how a member of the Mau Mau had confessed that he and three others had crept up to the car to kill the Higgenses, but when they saw the sixteen men surrounding the car, the Mau Mau left in fear. "Sixteen men?" Higgens responded. "I don't know what you mean!"
>
> While they were on furlough, a friend Clay Brent asked the Higgenses if they have been in any danger recently. Higgens asked, "Why?" Then Clay said that on March 23, God had placed a heavy prayer burden on his heart. He called the men of the church, and

sixteen of them met together and prayed until the burden lifted.[8]

In 2 Kings 6, we read the account of Elisha the prophet and his encounter with the king of Syria. He was incensed that his plans for attacks against the Israelites were being foiled by what he thought was a spy in his camp. In verses 11–13, we read:

> Therefore the heart of the king of Syria was greatly troubled by this thing; and he called his servants and said to them, "Will you not show me which of us is for the king of Israel?" And one of his servants said, "None, my lord, O king; but Elisha, the prophet who is in Israel, tells the king of Israel the words that you speak in your bedroom." So he said, "Go and see where he is, that I may send and get him." And it was told him, saying, "Surely he is in Dothan."

Imagine an entire army dispatched to bring in one lone prophet who had no visible means of protection! One morning, Elisha's servant was going about his daily duties when he glanced out a window and was stunned to see Syrian army forces camped around Dothan. He probably reacted much as we might have. He likely wrung his hands and cried out, "What to do? Oh, what to do?" Actually, according to verse 15, he said, "Alas, my master! What shall we do?"

Calmly, Elisha replied to his distraught servant:

> "Do not fear, for those who are with us are more than those who are with them." And Elisha prayed, and said, "LORD, I pray, open his eyes that he may see."

Then the LORD opened the eyes of the young man, and he saw. And behold, the mountain was full of horses and chariots of fire all around Elisha (vv. 16–17).

The servant was viewing the whole situation through earthly eyes. Danger surrounded him and his master. Death, he probably thought, was imminent. He was certain they were all going to die! But Elisha looked out the window with spiritual eyes and with confidence in the protection of Jehovah-Ganan—the Lord our Defense.

Psalm 91:11–12 reminds us:

For He shall give His angels charge over you, to keep you in all your ways. In their hands they shall bear you up, lest you dash your foot against a stone.

Then Elisha turned the tables on the Syrians. He asked not that their eyes be opened, but that they be blinded. But it didn't end there; no, Elisha led the troops into Samaria and presented them to their enemy. Imagine when they opened their eyes! They must surely have thought they were dead men walking.

When the king of Israel saw them, he said to Elisha, "Father, shall I massacre the lot?" "Not on your life!" said Elisha. "You didn't lift a hand to capture them, and now you're going to kill them? No sir, make a feast for them and send them back to their master."

So he prepared a huge feast for them. After they ate and drank their fill he dismissed them. Then they returned home to their master. The raiding bands of Aram didn't bother Israel anymore (2 Kings 6:21–23, MSG.)

I am reminded of the verse in Proverbs 25:21–22 that reads, "If your enemy is hungry, give him bread to eat; and if he is thirsty, give him water to drink; for so you will heap coals of fire on his head, and the LORD will reward you." And rewarded they were, for "The raiding bands of Aram didn't bother Israel anymore."

Elisha's servant was made fully aware of God's protection over His people. What a blessing and what joy there was in the Israelites' camp as their enemy was turned back, and God prevailed!

Storms do come to us even though we would much prefer that God hold them at bay. However, "Sometimes God calms the storm; sometimes He lets the storm rage and calms His child."[9] If you, like me, have ever seen God's profound protection during times of tremendous trouble, you have benefited from an unfathomable grasp of His divine protection that may have been missed had He simply spoke, "Peace, be still," to the storm. It is in these times that our faith is multiplied and we receive new and awe-inspiring awareness of God and His matchless love. God's mercy and shield are more than enough to keep us safe in the stormiest of situations. Just remember, "The eternal God is your refuge, and underneath are the everlasting arms" (Deuteronomy 33:27a).

When Moses and the children of Israel departed Egypt, the people had experienced firsthand Jehovah's defense during plague after plague. Finally they were on their way to the Promised Land. After six days on their journey, the Israelites faced yet another problem—a sea of water before them and an army of Egyptians in their rearview mirror. They were literally between the devil and the deep blue sea!

In abject fear they chided Moses for not leaving them in Egypt as slaves: "For it would have been better for us to serve the Egyptians than that we should die in the wilderness" (Exodus 14:12b). Moses assured them that God would protect His children: "Do not be afraid. Stand still, and see the salvation of the LORD, which He will accomplish for you today. For the Egyptians whom you see today, you shall see again no more forever. The LORD will fight for you, and you shall hold your peace" (vv. 13–14) In other words, "Shut up! Be still! God's in charge."

From the time God led them out of bondage He had guided and protected them with a cloud by day and a pillar of fire by night. As the multiplied hundreds of thousands of men, women, and children bedded down for the night, the cloud shifted from before them for direction to behind them for protection. It became a veil of darkness to the Egyptians and a huge night-light for the Israelites.

As sleep settled in over the multitudes, a strong east wind began to blow so that when morning dawned a thoroughfare of dry ground could be seen stretching from one side of the Red Sea to the other. As the call went out to move forward between the towering walls of water, the Israelites moved toward safety from the Egyptian army. Soon, Pharaoh's troops realized what was happening—their slaves were escaping—and set out in pursuit. But God had another surprise in store for the mighty army:

> Now it came to pass, in the morning watch, that the Lord looked down upon the army of the Egyptians through the pillar of fire and cloud, and He troubled the army of the Egyptians. And He took off their chariot wheels, so that they drove them with difficulty; and the Egyptians said, "Let us flee from the face of Israel, for the Lord fights for them against the Egyptians." Then the Lord said to Moses, "Stretch out your hand over the sea, that the waters may come

back upon the Egyptians, on their chariots, and on their horsemen." And Moses stretched out his hand over the sea; and when the morning appeared, the sea returned to its full depth, while the Egyptians were fleeing into it. So the Lord overthrew the Egyptians in the midst of the sea. Then the waters returned and covered the chariots, the horsemen, and all the army of Pharaoh that came into the sea after them. Not so much as one of them remained (Exodus 14:24–28).

Just as Moses had had favor with God that came from walking and communing with his heavenly Father, so did Jesus. That favor was sharpened by relationship and fellowship. He knew firsthand what He would later relay to the apostle Paul: "For I know whom I have believed and am persuaded that He is able to keep what I have committed to Him until that day" (2 Timothy 1:12). Jesus knew that His Father was fully able to keep that which had been committed unto Him. All we must do is dwell securely in that "secret place of the Most High" and protection and favor with God will be ours as His beloved children.

—DISCUSSION—
MATERIAL

1. Read Psalm 91.

2. Recall a time when you felt God's protection in your life.

3. Like the American Indian father in this chapter, have you ever stood guard in the background when someone in your life—perhaps a child—was trying his/her wings?

4. Do you suppose God still sends angels to guard His children? Why?

5. What might angels look like?

6. Can you think of other biblical instances of God sending angels to provide protection?

7. Why does God allow storms in our life?

8. Can you think of other Scriptures on God's protection?

—SCRIPTURES ON—
GOD'S PROTECTION

He who dwells in the secret place of the Most High shall abide under the shadow of the Almighty. I will say of the Lord, "He is my refuge and my fortress; my God, in Him I will trust." Surely He shall deliver you from the snare of the fowler and from the perilous pestilence. He shall cover you with His feathers, and under His wings you shall take refuge; His truth shall be your shield and buckler.
PSALM 91:1–4

A thousand may fall at your side, and ten thousand at your right hand; but it shall not come near you. Only with your eyes shall you look, and see the reward of the wicked.
PSALM 91:7–8

God is our refuge and strength, a very present help in trouble.
PSALM 46:1–2

You are my hiding place; You shall preserve me from trouble; You shall surround me with songs of deliverance.
PSALM 32:7

But let all those rejoice who put their trust in You; let them ever shout for joy, because You defend them; let those also who love Your name be joyful in You.
PSALM 5:11

Oh, taste and see that the Lord is good; blessed is the man who trusts in Him!
PSALM 34:8

I will abide in Your tabernacle forever;
I will trust in the shelter of Your wings.
PSALM 61:4

It is better to trust in the Lord than to put confidence in
man.
PSALM 118:8

My Father, who has given them to Me, is greater than all;
and no one is able to snatch them out of My Father's hand.
JOHN 10:29

Fear not, for I am with you; be not dismayed, for I am
your God. I will strengthen you, yes, I will help you, I will
uphold you with My righteous right hand.
ISAIAH 41:10

CHAPTER THREE

GOD'S GLORY

And he [Moses] said, "Please, show me Your glory."
EXODUS 33:18

WHEN I WAS ELEVEN, my father nearly killed me. In a fit
of rage at some perceived wrong, he grabbed me by the throat,
lifted me over his head, and applied pressure. The more I fought,
the tighter his grip became. As I looked into his face, I saw only
deadly rage. I was sure no father could hate a son more than he
hated me. I saw murder in his eyes. I could not breathe and began
to lose consciousness, certain my life was about to come to an end.
He tossed me on the floor in a broken heap. I crawled to the center
of the room, barely aware of my surroundings, gasping for every
breath. The pain was so intense that I scarcely remember heaving
up the contents of my stomach.

Sometime later I awoke, my body curled into a fetal position.
My face and pajamas were covered in dried vomit. My body ached.
I tried to push myself up from the floor of that dark room but fell
back, the room spinning. I closed my eyes, clenched my fists in total
agony, and shaking uncontrollably cried out, "Why was I born?

Why?!" I saw no purpose for my life. My father hated me, and all I knew was his warped version of Christianity. My dad's favorite Bible verse must have been Proverbs 23:14: "You shall beat him with a rod, and deliver his soul from hell." He paraphrased that as "Spare the rod, spoil the child." There were no spoiled children in his house—only abused ones. He had never given me one word of affirmation. Not once had I heard "I love you" from the lips that so tenderly and lovingly caressed a glass of amber whiskey. Jack Daniel's was his friend; I was "moron."

I finally managed to drag myself to the bed and dropped my head on my knees, closed my eyes, and whimpered again, "Why was I born?" As quickly as I had whispered those words, the room was flooded with a blinding light. I was terrified, thinking my dad had come back to finish the job. He was going to beat me to death, and this time I would not escape. I heard a noise that sounded like a wounded puppy's whine and realized the sound was coming from my own throat. My first thought was to crawl under the bed to protect myself from his steel-toed boots.

I covered my face with my hands and closed my eyes as tightly as I could squeeze them. After what seemed like an eon, I realized there was no other sound in the room, only the brilliant light. I slowly spread my fingers and eased my eyes open as imperceptibly as possible, hoping to see an empty room.

Instead I saw two hands reaching toward me. The palms were open, and in the center of each palm was an ugly scar. I had seen those hands in Sunday school literature. They were supposed to represent the nail scars in the hands of Jesus. Someone was playing a trick on me, but who? Did I dare look beyond the hands to the face? Had I gone crazy?

I opened my eyes wider and lifted my head slightly. Rather

than the cold, stark fear that had inhabited the room earlier, I now actually felt warmth. I felt a Presence that brought both power and peace. It was as if I were being immersed in an invisible liquid love that poured over me and lodged deep inside my soul. I slowly raised my head to see what was attached to those brilliantly luminous hands. As my eyes followed the arms upward, I saw standing there in my bedroom the Lord Jesus Christ. He was either clothed in light or in the most brilliant white imaginable--whiter than fresh snow; whiter than the clouds that floated in a sun-filled sky; whiter than anything I had ever seen. Draped from His shoulder to His waist was a deep purple cloth--more purple than the heavens at sunset.

As I lifted my head to take in His face, I was instantly drawn to His loving eyes. They were smiling, happy eyes filled with every color of the rainbow. It was like looking into an illuminated bowl of the world's most highly prized jewels. I felt as if I could see through those eyes and beyond to heaven and the promise of eternal peace.

Keeping His arms outstretched, He looked at me with such an expression of love. He smiled and then said three things I had never heard before. They were like a healing salve to my wounded soul and spirit.

He said, *"Son."* It was the first time anyone had ever called me Son. It was said so gently, with such love and respect for me--for me!—that I felt my heart melt. The word *son* echoed in my spirit again and again.

"I love you." Someone really did love me. What joy! I felt as if I'd just escaped a death sentence and was free. That statement alone was enough to sustain me for the rest of my life. But He continued, *"I have a great plan for your life."* The glory of God was like a holy fire igniting my soul. I had a purpose! God had something for me to do. Then there was silence. I am sure only a few seconds had

passed, but it felt like an eternity. I closed my eyes, and tears slid slowly down my face. I was consumed with an inexplicable joy. Eventually I realized that the glory had departed but the overwhelming warmth remained. He was gone from my room but not from my being, not from my heart.

The Hebrew word for glory is *kabod*. Its original meaning is "weight" or "heaviness." It literally means "to be important," and the same word is interchangeable with honor and majesty. I felt the full weight of God's kabod in my room that night all those years ago.

In 1 Samuel 4, we read the account of one of the children of Israel's blackest hours. The nation had been overpowered by their archenemy, the Philistines. The priests in Israel, including Eli, the High Priest and his son, Phineas, had been put to death and the Ark of the Covenant had been taken by the adversary. When the news of the death of her husband and father-in-law reached the wife of Phineas, she went into labor and bore a son whom she named Icabod, meaning "the glory of God has departed."

Two noteworthy incidents took place in the period that led to Israel's downfall and the capture of the Ark: disobedience and a loss of leadership. First it was said of Eli's sons, Hophni and Phineas, that they made the Lord's people transgress (see 1 Samuel 2:24). The two men entertained prostitutes inside the Temple and profited from those who offered sacrifices at Shiloh. The two also failed to keep the lamps in the Temple full of oil so their flame would not be extinguished.

Even before judgment was pronounced on Eli and his sons, God was preparing a child, one born to preach a message of redemption to Jehovah's wandering children. In the first chapter of 1 Samuel, a heartbroken and barren woman made her way to the Temple to offer a sacrifice and pray. She pleaded with God to grant her request for a child. Hannah covenanted with Jehovah to rear her son only until he was old enough to be weaned from her breast and then to present the child to the Lord for service in the Temple. Out of Hannah's despair, God raised up a righteous prophet—Samuel—to serve Him.

First Samuel 3:1–4 declares:

> Now the boy Samuel ministered to the LORD before Eli. And the word of the LORD was rare in those days; there was no widespread revelation. And it came to pass at that time, while Eli was lying down in his place, and when his eyes had begun to grow so dim that he could not see, and before the lamp of God went out in the tabernacle of the LORD where the ark of God was, and while Samuel was lying down, that the LORD called Samuel. And he answered, "Here I am!"

Just as God had not abandoned Hannah, just as He heard her prayer, so He also heard the prayer of the righteous that remained in Israel. Jehovah had a faultless strategy and flawless timing with which to raise up His people and restore righteousness in the land. God desires that His people experience His glory; He wants us to have favor with Him.

We read in Exodus 33:18 that Moses asked of God, "Please, show me Your glory." What an audacious request Moses had made of God! God, who has promised to hear and answer our cries, must have been saddened by such an appeal. It seems to be verified by His response to Moses in verse 20: "But He said, 'You cannot see My face; for no man shall see Me, and live.'" God, however, had a plan to grant Moses' petition.

Moses had experienced the presence of God as manifested in the plagues that beset the Egyptians before the children of Israel were allowed to leave Egypt. He had seen the pillar of fire at night and the cloud during the day while he led the Israelites through the wilderness toward the Promised Land. He had great faith in the ability of God to take care of His children. And yet, because of his relationship with Jehovah, Moses asked for an even more intimate experience: He wanted to see, firsthand, the glory of God. It was the supreme appeal that he could have made: "Show me Your glory."

Moses is the only man in the Bible to have made such a simple yet dynamic request, and with it, he stood head and shoulders above all other Bible characters. It was surely the sincere longing behind the petition that touched the heart of God and moved His hand to grant the desire of Moses' heart. He had favor with God, and the Creator of the universe responded. How did Moses feel after he had made such a bold appeal? Did he tremble at the audacity of his entreaty? Did he quake in his sandals? Did the hair on the back of his neck stand up at such boldness? Moses had a sustained track record of favor with God. He knew Jehovah to be faithful. He had seen His glory in the burning bush, in the fire and cloud, in the parting of the waters of the Red Sea, in the salvation of an entire people during the solemn Passover. Moses was sustained by both faith and favor; he knew his God. Like Daniel, he must have thought, "but the people who know their God shall be strong, and carry out *great exploits*" (*Daniel 11:32b*). Or as we might say, "Nothing ventured; nothing gained."

Moses' favor with God had been earned in the fire of adversity and the cloud of spiritual union. The leader of the children of Israel had pitched a tent outside the camp. Exodus 33:7b–11a tells us:

> And it came to pass that everyone who sought the
> LORD went out to the tabernacle of meeting which was
> outside the camp. So it was, whenever Moses went
> out to the tabernacle, that all the people rose, and
> each man stood at his tent door and watched Moses
> until he had gone into the tabernacle. And it came to
> pass, when Moses entered the tabernacle, that the
> pillar of cloud descended and stood at the door of the
> tabernacle, and the LORD talked with Moses. All the
> people saw the pillar of cloud standing at the taberna-
> cle door, and all the people rose and worshiped, each
> man in his tent door. So the LORD spoke to Moses face
> to face, as a man speaks to his friend.

He need not fear a close encounter with Jehovah; he knew that
he had purified himself and was prepared for the meeting. Moses
refused to allow fear to rob him of stepping into the very presence
of Jehovah. As the apostle Paul wrote in 1 John 4:18: "There is no
fear in love; but perfect love casts out fear, because fear involves
torment."

In verse Exodus 33:13, Moses petitions God to "show me now
Your way, that I may know You." He wanted to *know* the way of
God, before he requested to *see* the glory of God. He established a
bond before he sought a glimpse of the Almighty. Moses was not
a beggar who had to grovel at the back door of the throne room,
seeking but not expecting an audience with the Lord of the manor.
No, he was a son who had access to the front entrance, an open door
because he had favor with God.

In Isaiah 6:1, the prophet had a vision:

In the year that King Uzziah died, I saw the Lord sitting on a throne, high and lifted up, and the train of His robe filled the temple.

Moses had an encounter with the Creator and Sustainer, a personal encounter:

And the LORD said, "Here is a place by Me, and you shall stand on the rock. So it shall be, while My glory passes by, that I will put you in the cleft of the rock, and will cover you with My hand while I pass by. Then I will take away My hand, and you shall see My back; but My face shall not be seen" (Exodus 33:21–23).

A place by God, covered by His hand—cherished, protected, blessed, and highly favored! Moses saw, not the God of judgment, not the all-consuming fire; he basked in the presence of a God who loved the man He had chosen to lead His people, the one upon whom rested favor with God. The great preacher Charles Spurgeon wrote in his sermon "A View of God's Glory":

Then, again, it is true that *no man, even as a saint, can see God's face and live;* not because of moral disability, but because of physical inability. The body is not strong enough to bear the sight or vision of God.... This much is certain—that on earth, no man, however holy, can ever see God's face, and yet live.[10]

As Moses peeked between his fingers at God from his hiding

place in the cleft of the rock, his senses were consumed by the glory of the Creator; his heart was filled with awe for the character and power of Jehovah; and he was transformed by the overwhelming love of God.

The picture of Moses hidden in the cleft of the rock is a perfect illustration of favor with God. We have been placed in Christ Jesus by God the Father. We have been adopted as His child into a place where His glory is revealed and we can in perfect trust experience the glory of Jehovah's love for us. In Exodus 33:19, God reveals what we can expect as His child:

> Then He said, "I will make all My goodness pass before you, and I will proclaim the name of the LORD before you. I will be gracious to whom I will be gracious, and I will have compassion on whom I will have compassion."

God was not obligated to allow Moses to see His glory; it was because God had poured out His grace freely and Moses had found favor in the eyes of the Lord. Moses was allowed to see the glory of Jehovah, not so he could boast of his relationship, but so that he might be transformed. When Jesus "became flesh and dwelt among us, and we beheld His glory, the glory as of the only begotten of the Father, full of grace and truth" (John 1:14), it was for the express purpose of redeeming mankind so that we might be transformed into His image. Jesus exhibited "all the fullness of the Godhead bodily" (Colossians 2:9)—mercy, grace, forgiveness, love, joy, peace. In the gift of Jesus Christ, God the Father wrapped up everything He is and everything He wants us to be. Paul reminded the Corinthian Believers of this in 2 Corinthians 3:18:

But we all, with unveiled face, beholding as in a mirror the glory of the Lord, are being transformed into the same image from glory to glory, just as by the Spirit of the Lord.

Our lives are to be revolutionized by the glory of God. In Ephesians 1:18, Paul admonishes the Believer:

The eyes of your understanding being enlightened; that you may know what is the hope of His calling, what are the riches of the glory of His inheritance in the saints...

Jehovah revealed His glory to Moses so that his eyes might be opened to just who God was—not simply a God of vengeance as he had seen visited on the Egyptians—but a God of love; a God whose power and presence were intertwined and inseparable from His glory.

Paul continued in Ephesians 3:14–19:

For this reason I bow my knees to the Father of our Lord Jesus Christ, from whom the whole family in heaven and earth is named, that He would grant you, according to the riches of His glory, to be strengthened with might through His Spirit in the inner man, that Christ may dwell in your hearts through faith; that you, being rooted and grounded in love, may be able to comprehend with all the saints what *is* the width and length and depth and height—to know the

love of Christ which passes knowledge; that you may
be filled with all the fullness of God.

Just as the revelation of God's glory became so real to Moses, so
it should be in the life of the Believer until that knowledge changes
us into the man or woman God desires us to be. We must continue
to study the Word of God, to seek to see His glory until we are
changed as Paul said in 2 Corinthians 3:18, "from glory to glory, just
as by the Spirit of the Lord."

—DISCUSSION—
MATERIAL

1. Read Exodus 33.

2. How can we see God's glory
   in the world around us?

3. Remember an instance when you
   were particularly awed by a display
   of God's creation.

4. Eli allowed his sons to run wild.
   What is the responsibility of a
   parent to train up a child?

5. How can a parent accomplish such
   training?

6. Share an experience from your own
   life on how you provided direction
   to your children.

7. Why do you think God showed
   Moses His glory?

8. Are we today too causal in our
   approach to God in worship?

—SCRIPTURES ON—
GOD'S GLORY

Whether therefore ye eat, or drink, or whatsoever ye do, do all to the glory of God.
1 Corinthians 10:31 kjv

Who being the brightness of his glory, and the express image of his person, and upholding all things by the word of his power, when he had by himself purged our sins, sat down on the right hand of the Majesty on high:
Hebrews 1:3 kjv

Jesus saith unto her, Said I not unto thee, that, if thou wouldest believe, thou shouldest see the glory of God?
John 11:40 kjv

For all have sinned, and come short of the glory of God;
Romans 3:23 kjv

And the sight of the glory of the Lord was like devouring fire on the top of the mount in the eyes of the children of Israel.
Exodus 24:17 kjv

But ye shall be named the Priests of the Lord: men shall call you the Ministers of our God: ye shall eat the riches of the Gentiles, and in their glory shall ye boast yourselves.
Isaiah 61:6 kjv

O Lord, our Lord, how excellent is thy name in all the earth! who hast set thy glory above the heavens.
Psalm 8:1 kjv

And that every tongue should confess that Jesus Christ is Lord, to the glory of God the Father.
Philippians 2:11 kjv

To whom God would make known what is the riches of the glory of this mystery among the Gentiles; which is Christ in you, the hope of glory:

COLOSSIANS 1:27 KJV

CHAPTER FOUR

GOD'S BLESSING

*Now it shall come to pass, if you diligently obey the
voice of the Lord your God, to observe carefully all His
commandments which I command you today, that the Lord
your God will set you high above all nations of the earth.
And all these blessings shall come upon you and overtake
you, because you obey the voice of the Lord your God:*

DEUTERONOMY 28:1–2

IN 1983, MY BELOVED WIFE, CAROLYN, and I already
had three beautiful daughters. One day she came to me in tears
and said, "God spoke to me and told me that we would have a son
who would be a mighty man of God." I took her statement very
seriously, as she rarely said that God spoke to her. Several months
later, she informed me that she was pregnant. "This is a boy," she
said.

During the pregnancy Carolyn had two sonograms and both
times was told she was carrying a girl. She replied very strongly, "I
am not; it's a boy!" On July 17, 1984, Michael was born. As I cut the
umbilical cord, I lifted him above his mother's womb and dedicated
him to the Lord.

Later when I walked down to the nursery to look through the window at our son, I saw that the name on the bassinet read "Michael David Evans II." I had no middle name; I was simply named "Michael Evans." I went back to Carolyn's room and asked, "Honey, how can he be Michael David the second? I'm not Michael David the first."

Her response was, "God told me to name him that. Now it's your problem to resolve."

Not long afterward, I sat in a courtroom before a judge to have my name changed to Michael David Evans. There were others in the room when the judge asked me, "Why do you want to change your name?"

I responded, "I want to be named after my son." The judge smiled as many occupants in the courtroom burst into laughter. Today, what a blessing to have seen Michael David Evans II mature into a dedicated man of God, husband, and father—a son to delight and bless any dad.

In Deuteronomy 28, Moses stood before the children of Israel and delivered a message of blessing from Jehovah to the assembly. He knew above all that future stability rested solely in their union with Yahweh. They had been miraculously delivered from Egypt and shielded and sustained during their forty-year sojourn in the desert. Now they stood on the banks of the Jordan River, about to enter the Promised Land. Although God had shown them time after time that blessings came by His hand, Moses had been given the task of reminding them, of impressing that lesson indelibly in their minds. Their leader could not bless them; the priests of Levi could not bless them; the most devout among their number could not bless them; that fell to God alone. While the Levites could intone:

"The LORD bless you and keep you; the LORD make His face shine upon you, and be gracious to you; the LORD lift up His countenance upon you, and give you peace" (Numbers 6:24–26), only God could infuse the blessing with action. Only He could exalt; only He could redeem His people, Israel.

In Ephesians 3:20, the apostle Paul wrote:

> Now to Him who is able to do exceedingly abundantly above all that we ask or think, according to the power that works in us ...

Paul knew that God is able to do all things if we but believe Him for the blessing. Too often we find it easier to fall prey to the Enemy, who is in all things depraved, immoral and spiteful, rather than fully trusting in the blessings of a benevolent, loving, patient, and righteous heavenly Father. The Believer tends to forget that in Matthew 7:11, Jesus described God's love for His children in this way:

> If you then, being evil, know how to give good gifts to your children, how much more will your Father who is in heaven give good things to those who ask Him!

The psalmist wrote in chapter 84, verses 11–12:

> For the LORD God is a sun and shield; the LORD will give grace and glory; no good thing will He withhold from those who walk uprightly. O LORD of hosts, blessed *is* the man who trusts in You!

When Jesus sat down on a grassy knoll with His followers, He delivered His first discourse (what Christians call the Beatitudes) designed to characterize the qualities of a true Believer in Matthew 5:3–12:

> "Blessed are the poor in spirit, for theirs is the kingdom of heaven. Blessed are those who mourn, for they shall be comforted. Blessed are the meek, for they shall inherit the earth. Blessed are those who hunger and thirst for righteousness, for they shall be filled. Blessed are the merciful, for they shall obtain mercy. Blessed are the pure in heart, for they shall see God. Blessed are the peacemakers, for they shall be called sons of God. Blessed are those who are persecuted for righteousness' sake, for theirs is the kingdom of heaven. Blessed are you when they revile and persecute you, and say all kinds of evil against you falsely for My sake. Rejoice and be exceedingly glad, for great is your reward in heaven, for so they persecuted the prophets who were before you."

The Greek word translated as "blessed" or "happy" is *makarios*. It was a very common word in Jesus' day, but He used it to express a very uncommon state; He purported that those not normally considered blessed—the poor in spirit, the hungry and thirsty, or the persecuted—were truly makarios. In daily usage it was thought that the rich were blessed, the privileged were happy, and the distinguished and famous were fortunate. Jesus might have said something like, "Not by a long shot!" In his book *Simple Faith*, Charles Swindoll wrote of the Sermon on the Mount:

Having endured a lifetime of verbal assaults by the scribes and Pharisees, the multitude on the mount must have thought they had died and gone to heaven.[11]

In his book *The Beatitudes, The Only Way to Happiness*, Dr. John MacArthur wrote of how the world views happiness:

The world says: "Happy is the go-getter, the guy who pushes everyone else out of his way, the guy who gets what he wants when he wants it, where he wants it, and how he wants it. Happiness is macho. Happiness is doing your own thing. Happiness is grabbing all the gusto you can get. Happiness is acquiring. Happy are the rich, happy are the noble, happy are the famous, and happy are the popular." ... The very start of the Sermon on the Mount tells us the whole point—that we should know real blessedness, real happiness, real joy, real gladness, genuine bliss, and divine reward.[12]

The Beatitudes present a picture of what the life of the Believer should be when we allow God to live in and through us. That is what the Beatitudes are about—God showing through. It has always been God's purpose that when He entered our lives, He would be allowed to so fill and control us that He would "show through"—that He would be visible in our manners and mannerisms. We should not simply pretend to be what God has called us to be, but Christ should shine through our transparent lives...like a lamp that only glows when connected to a power source.

The truth is, we can't simply "act" our way through life. There is no way we can achieve God's purpose and receive God's abundant blessings if we are simply playing a role. The Father wants the world to see, not us, but the image of His Son shining through us.

Late country star Porter Wagoner sang a song with lyrics by Red Sovine, "If Jesus Came to Your House." As the title suggests, it questions how our lives would change if Jesus came to "spend a day or two." The song ends:

> Would you be glad to have him stay forever
> > on and on
> Or would you sigh with great relief when he at last
> > was gone
> It might be interesting to know the things that
> > you would do
> If Jesus came in person to spend some time
> > with you.[13]

Would it be a burden or a blessing if Jesus came to your house? How would your activities differ from every other day? Would it change the way you treat others? Conduct business? Live your life? Yet we boast that Jesus lives within us, and that is precisely what He desires to do. When we pause to consider that the Beatitudes are a picture of the attributes of Christ, we should lay aside Self and allow Him to develop those characteristics in our lives. We should live every day with the knowledge that Jesus *has* come to reside in our "earthly houses."

Let's take a brief look at the attributes and attitudes He wants to develop in His children. First, Jesus was poor in spirit. Does that mean material lack? Does it mean shedding ourselves of everything we own or ever hope to own in order to meet Jesus' criteria? No, He's not referring to physical poverty, but poverty of spirit. While that doesn't sound like a very good place to be, one important clue can be found in James 4:10:

> Humble yourselves in the sight of the Lord, and
> He will lift you up.

Another is evident in Jesus' parable of the Pharisee and the tax collector in Luke 18:10–14:

> Two men went up to the temple to pray, one a Pharisee and the other a tax collector. The Pharisee stood and prayed thus with himself, "God, I thank You that I am not like other men—extortioners, unjust, adulterers, or even as this tax collector. I fast twice a week; I give tithes of all that I possess." And the tax collector, standing afar off, would not so much as raise *his* eyes to heaven, but beat his breast, saying, "God, be merciful to me a sinner!" I tell you, this man went down to his house justified *rather* than the other; for everyone who exalts himself will be humbled, and he who humbles himself will be exalted.

God is near those whose spirits cry out to Him in total dependence. The psalmist wrote in chapter 51, verse 17 of a "broken spirit, a broken and a contrite heart." The poor in spirit are men and women who recognize their need for a Savior and cry out as did the tax collector, "God be merciful to me." Pride has been shattered, replaced by a meek and repentant spirit. Realizing their own total weakness, Believers can now reach out to Jehovah for everything, and in surrendering find favor with God.

There are other prominent examples in the Scriptures of men who found favor with God because they were poor in spirit. Moses threw himself at the feet of Yahweh when he walked up to a burning bush in the desert. When asked to take up his staff and free the children of Israel from bondage, his first response was, "Lord, I'm too inadequate to undertake such a massive task." Moses knew he could do nothing within himself; anything accomplished would be by the hand of God Almighty. The Lord of the wilderness assured Moses that with Him all things were possible (see Matthew 19:26).

As we read in chapter one, Gideon was challenged to rescue Israel from the grip of its Midianite oppressors. This son of Joash was certain he could do nothing, for he said, "O my Lord, how can I save Israel? Indeed my clan *is* the weakest in Manasseh, and I *am* the least in my father's house" (Judges 6:15). God responded by calling Gideon a "mighty man of valor." In the midst of his confessed incapability, Jehovah assured Gideon that he could get the job done with the help of the One who never slumbers or sleeps. The plan was laid out, and Gideon, totally relying on God for strength and direction, brought it to fruition—not my might, nor by power, but by the Spirit of the Lord of hosts (see Zechariah 4:6).

Isaiah was another man of God who realized he was nothing in himself. In Isaiah 6, he was transported in a vision into the throne room of the Almighty. Isaiah saw the temple filled with the train of Jehovah's robe—He who sits high and lifted up. It was then that the prophet realized his own humanity, for he cried out in Isaiah 6:5:

> Woe *is* me, for I am undone! Because I *am* a man
> of unclean lips, and I dwell in the midst of a people

of unclean lips; for my eyes have seen the King, The
LORD of hosts.

It was in that moment of poverty of spirit that God was able to
send Isaiah forth on a mission to minister to the children of Israel.
These are but a few of the many men and women recorded in the
Bible who at some juncture placed their total dependence on God,
and were then available to be used by Him.

Among those blessed abundantly by God, one of the lesser
known is Ezra, a priest exiled in Babylon. He was, according to
chapter 7, verse 6, "a skilled scribe in the Law of Moses." Verse 9
reminds us that Ezra had "the good hand of his God upon him."
According to verse 10 and reiterated in others in the chapter, this
was because, "Ezra had prepared his heart to seek the Law of the
LORD, and to do it, and to teach statutes and ordinances in Israel."
There is a certain connection between the Believer's faithfulness to
understand and submit to the Word of God, and Jehovah's blessings
that fall on us.

After he petitioned King Artaxerxes to be allowed to return to
Jerusalem and was granted permission, God blessed Ezra exceedingly abundantly more than Ezra could have imagined. He was
given authorization to travel to Jerusalem to teach the Scriptures
to the Jewish people residing there:

> ✧ funds to purchase provisions and have the
> utensils used in Temple worship recreated;

> ✧ as much as 3 ¾ tons of silver, 600 bushels of
> wheat; 600 gallons of wine; 600 gallons of
> olive oil; and as much salt as was required;

- ✧ exemption from taxation for those who worked in the Temple;

- ✧ authority to establish a legal system and mete out punishment as required.

Doubtless, this was vastly more than Ezra could have imagined of a heathen ruler. Again, I'm reminded of Ephesians 3:20, "Now to Him who is able to do exceedingly abundantly above all that we ask or think." After reading the missive from the king, Ezra's response was one of praise:

> Blessed be the LORD God of our fathers, who has put such a thing as this in the king's heart, to beautify the house of the LORD which is in Jerusalem (Ezra 7:27).

Ezra was blessed beyond measure because he had favor with God. When Ezra finally set foot in Jerusalem after a long and arduous journey, he discovered that conditions in Judah were terribly disheartening. God's Word was generally ignored; few were vigilant concerning religious matters; and moral standards were at an all-time low. Many of the Israelites had married gentiles, a practice that was forbidden by Jehovah and threatened death to those who capitulated to pagan deities. He began to preach the Word of God to the people and the result was revival and return to the precepts of Jehovah. Blessing and favor with God was the result.

There are those who view serving God as a negative. If you ask, they will gladly list all that is forbidden to the Christian. They single out the "thou shalt nots" instead of the blessings that pursue the

Believer. It sounds as if God is playing a game of "Whac-A-Mole" and we are the mole. Nothing could be further from the truth.

Jesus delivered a sermon to His followers that painted a diametrically opposed picture of Yahweh—a God who wanted His followers to be blessed. His desire was to see them live a life filled with contentment, happiness, and enjoyment. British Bible scholar Dr. G. Campbell Morgan wrote:

> "Blessed" is therefore a condition—such a condition as to create a consciousness, which is the consciousness of a perfect peace, and a perfect joy, and a perfect rest. All these things are included in the condition of Happiness!
>
> That is God's will for man. That is the Divine intention for human life. Sorrow and sighing are to flee away; He will wipe away all tears. Happiness and joy are never to flee away; He will never banish merriment and laughter.
>
> So, a happy word is the first word of the Manifesto. It is a word full of sunshine, thrilling with music, brimming over with just what man is seeking after in a thousand false ways.[14]

The world says we are blessed when we are rich, powerful, intelligent, and/or famous. God says we are rich when we empty ourselves at the foot of the cross; when we realize, as did John the Baptist, that He must increase and we must decrease (see John 3:30).

We began this chapter in the book of Deuteronomy, where Moses listed for the people assembled the ways God would bless them if they followed Him, if they walked in His word and precepts.

The list of blessings is long, and can be safeguarded by a life of obedience and surrender. While God's love is unconditional, the abundance of His blessings is tied to Believers by the smallest of threads: the word *if*.

> *If* you fully obey the LORD your God and carefully follow all his commands I give you today, the LORD your God will set you high above all the nations on earth. All these blessings will come on you and accompany you *if* you obey the LORD your God (Deuteronomy 28:1–2 NIV, emphasis mine).

While He still loves us through our rebellion, He holds no obligation to bless us in our sins. That would be a total breach of His character. Obedience is the key to reaping the blessings of God in the life of the Believer. When we live a life that is pleasing to God, Proverbs says, "He makes even his enemies to be at peace with him" (Proverbs 16:7).

In Ephesians 1:3, the apostle Paul reminds us that God's blessings are not just physical, but, he writes: "Blessed be the God and Father of our Lord Jesus Christ, who has blessed us with every spiritual blessing in the heavenly places in Christ ..."

Another blessing is found in Galatians 4:7: "Therefore you are no longer a slave but a son, and if a son, then an heir of God through Christ." And yet another in Ephesians 1:7: "In Him we have redemption through His blood, the forgiveness of sins, according to the riches of His grace." What precious promises from our Lord!

Equally important is that we have not been blessed to sit; we have been blessed to serve. We have not been blessed to store; we have been blessed to share. In Genesis 12:2, God pronounces a mighty blessing over Abraham:

> I will make you a great nation; I will bless you and make your name great; and *you shall be a blessing* (emphasis mine).

A stream with no outlet stagnates and becomes useless. A Believer who hoards blessings becomes stagnant, ineffective, and lazy. To be an effective ambassador for Christ, we must be a channel for His blessings that flow through us to others. What can we do to become a dynamic Believer? We can find a need and fill it by offering emotional or financial support, or simply offering practical help.

It should not be our reason for offering assistance, but God has promised to return blessing for blessing. In Luke 6:38, Jesus says:

> "Give, and it will be given to you: good measure, pressed down, shaken together, and running over will be put into your bosom. For with the same measure that you use, it will be measured back to you."

In *The Life God Blesses*, author Jim Cymbala wrote:

> Kingdom joy and kingdom blessings are not measured in terms of affluence, mirth, pleasure, abundance, and ease. In fact, the *spiritual* qualities that reap kingdom blessings are incompatible with this world's values.
>
> So the citizen of God's kingdom is not *supposed* to feel at home in this world. Our citizenship belongs to

the heavenly kingdom, and we are but strangers and sojourners in this world—put here to serve as ambassadors of the King. As such, we are to live under the higher standards of the heavenly kingdom—and we also reap its infinitely higher privileges.[15]

In Matthew 10, Jesus delivers the charge of service to His disciples. In verse 8, He admonishes them: "Freely you have received, freely give." This is the commandment He delivers today to those whom He has so richly blessed with His favor.

—DISCUSSION—
MATERIAL

1. Read Matthew 5.

2. Do you know Jesus lives in you?

3. How should our daily conduct change with that knowledge?

4. Isaiah was overwhelmed by the majesty of God in chapter 6. Have you been in a worship service where you could feel the holy presence of Almighty God?

5. Ezra had favor with God and man. Think of an experience when you felt you had favor with God.

6. How do you picture God—as a loving heavenly Father or as a tyrant?

7. What are some of God's blessings in your life?

8. Make a list of your blessings, and this week in your prayer time, take a moment to thank God for His blessings to you.

—SCRIPTURES ON—
GOD'S BLESSINGS

A faithful man shall abound with blessings, but he who makes haste to be rich [at any cost] shall not go unpunished.
PROVERBS 28:20 AMP

And as you have been a curse and a byword among the nations, O house of Judah and house of Israel, so will I save you, and you shall be a blessing. Fear not, but let your hands be strong and hardened.
ZECHARIAH 8:13 AMP

Salvation belongs to the Lord; May Your blessing be upon Your people.
PSALM 3:8 AMP

For You send blessings of good things to meet him; You set a crown of pure gold on his head.
PSALM 21:3 AMP

For You make him to be blessed and a blessing forever; You make him exceedingly glad with the joy of Your presence.
PSALM 21:6 AMP

Out of the same mouth come forth blessing and cursing. These things, my brethren, ought not to be so.
JAMES 3:10 AMP

That the blessing of Abraham might come upon the Gentiles in Christ Jesus, that we might receive the promise of the Spirit through faith.
GALATIANS 3:14

Yes, he loved cursing, and it came [back] upon him; he delighted not in blessing, and it was far from him.
PSALM 109:17 AMP

Behold, I set before you this day a blessing and a curse—the blessing if you obey the commandments of the Lord your God which I command you this day.

DEUTERONOMY 11:26–27 AMP

Nevertheless, the Lord your God would not listen to Balaam, but the Lord your God turned the curse into a blessing to you, because the Lord your God loves you.

DEUTERONOMY 23:5 AMP

CHAPTER FIVE

GOD'S GLADNESS
AND REJOICING

*"The Lord your God in your midst, the Mighty One, will
save; He will rejoice over you with gladness, He will quiet
you with His love, He will rejoice over you with singing."*

ZEPHANIAH 3:17

HAD I READ THIS VERSE IN MY YOUTH, I would never
have believed it could be possible that anyone, let alone God, would
rejoice over me with gladness and singing. As I mentioned earlier,
my childhood was filled with abuse by an alcoholic father who
loved his whiskey more than his family. That was what spurred
me to enlist in the army at the age of seventeen.

After completing the paperwork for induction, the sergeant
asked, "Now, before you leave, tell me: Do you have any idea where
you'd like to be stationed?" I looked on the map that was posted
on the wall of the recruiter's office and tried to find the farthest
possible place from my father. There were pushpins in the map to
indicate where US Army troops were stationed. There it was! A tiny
rectangle: South Korea. Although the Korean Conflict had officially
ended in 1953, the United States still had troops stationed along the

demilitarized zone to deter the North Koreans from slipping across the border. That's where I wanted to go.

As a soldier, I spent fourteen months in South Korea on a mountain the Koreans called Wonton-ni. Wandering around the mountain early one morning, I experienced the overwhelming presence of God settling over me, flooding me with the burning desire to be a man of righteousness and integrity. Joy unspeakable filled my soul, and like Samuel of old, my spirit whispered, "Speak, Lord, for thy servant heareth" (see 1 Samuel 3:10 KJV). Finding a secluded spot, I sank to the ground and tears rained down my face as the Holy Spirit gently reminded me of Jesus' words when He had appeared to me as a child.

I whispered, "Jesus, will you ever talk to me audibly again? I need to hear Your voice. I sense the same presence I did when I was eleven." He did not answer me clearly, but suddenly I felt impressed by the Holy Spirit to turn to Daniel 10:9–11. With tears still misting my eyes, I read:

> Yet I heard the sound of his words; and while I heard the sound of his words I was in a deep sleep on my face, with my face to the ground. Suddenly, a hand touched me, which made me tremble on my knees and on the palms of my hands. And he said to me, "O Daniel, man greatly beloved, understand the words that I speak to you, and stand upright, for I have now been sent to you."

While He was speaking this word to my spirit, I stood trembling and weeping. I had run as far as I could from my earthly father only to fall securely into the arms of my heavenly Father. Eventually, the sensation of God's presence lifted, but His peace continued to surround me.

The Spirit of God I had just experienced on that mountain was the same presence I had encountered in my bedroom—first the presence, then the voice. Now I had experienced His presence, but where was His voice? I wanted to walk uprightly before my God, and I craved His spoken direction.

Before leaving the spot that day, I gathered twelve stones and set up a small altar. Sometime during the day, every day, I returned to that spot to pray and seek God.

As it had with my childhood encounter with Jesus, my life changed. I would never again be the same. I was loved; I was celebrated; I was cherished by my heavenly Father. It totally changed the picture I had of God. No longer was He a figure on the cross in the Catholic church down the street. No longer was He some vague, elusive Spirit about whom the Sunday school teacher told improbable stories. No longer was He aloof, unconcerned, unfeeling, and uncaring. Now He was a loving, compassionate, involved Father who, I would later learn, rejoiced over me with gladness and singing!

On that fateful evening atop Wonton-ni only the presence of a Holy God could have soothed my hungry soul and spirit. Back then I could only wallow in His love and kindness. Now I can rejoice that not only does God love me, but He's glad I'm His child, and I can but wonder what the words might be to the love song He sings just for me.

As we examine Zephaniah 3:17, we find there are five distinct segments that present a remarkable glimpse into the very heart of our Father:

1. His presence
2. His power to save
3. His love
4. His peace
5. His song

What joy! The Father is delighted with you. His love for you is never-ending and never failing. As one pastor wrote:

> It doesn't matter if you are struggling, your attitude is terrible, you are depressed, divorced and disappointed, God delights in you. It doesn't matter if you are caught up in a pity party, your friends have abandoned you, your kids are a mess and your job is a disaster. God delights in you so much He is singing.[16]

The Hebrew word *rinnah* means "a ringing cry; a joyful shout." That is what rings forth from the throne room when your life is especially pleasing to Jehovah. Can you imagine God picking you up and swinging you round and round, all the while laughing with abandon at the success of His child?

When you are wounded and hurting, picture a mother drawing her child to her breast and whispering a lullaby to soothe the distraught baby. That is the heavenly Father—calmly and quietly nurturing you and me in our distress. Sit silently before the Lord; can you hear the song of rejoicing He is singing over you? Can you feel His peace as it steals over you, calming your spirit? That sweet presence surrounding you is the omnipresent Father. The Lord of the universe, the God of all Creation, El Elyon—the God Most High—is delighted with you. He "quiets you with His love" and "rejoices over you with singing."

The purpose of the book of Zephaniah was to deliver a letter of hope to the Israelites who were surrounded by an impossible situation—to bring hope when all seemed lost. The prophet was anointed to paint a picture with words to a discouraged and depressed people. His message: All is not lost. God knows you and loves you! Listen closely and hear His song of deliverance.

Pastor Dr. Neil Chadwick wrote:

> If heaven is "up", then right now God the Father is looking "down" upon us, and there is a smile on His face and mirth in His eyes. And even now He is preparing the party of the ages; soon He will send out the call in the words of Matthew 25:21, "enter into the joy of your Lord." Yes, in this life we know sorrow and heartache, but remember, "weeping may remain for a night, but rejoicing comes in the morning" (Psalm 30:5).[17]

Why? Because God is a God of joy, and we are invited to enter into His joy! We have become Believers with benefits—forgiveness, faith, and a future with Him in eternity. Judgment has been replaced with joy; hell has given way to heaven; struggle has been supplanted with serenity. Yes, my friend, Almighty God rejoices over you with gladness!

When a need arises, the Believer does not have to crawl on his belly to seek an audience with the King of Kings. No, as His child, we have access to our Father's throne room anytime. I'm reminded of the picture of John F. Kennedy, Jr. as a child playing under his father's desk in the Oval Office of the White House. Others had to make appointments, sometimes months in advance, but John-John had access to his father because of sonship. Just as his father's face was filled with joy when his little boy peeked around the door into his office, so our heavenly Father's face is filled with gladness when we come "boldly before the throne of grace" (see Hebrews 4:16).

I believe the principal response in God's presence is gladness. In Psalm 16:11, David said, "In Your presence is fullness of joy; at Your right hand are pleasures forevermore." In the presence of the Father is eternal gladness for all eternity. In Acts chapter 2, Peter stood before a crowd and preached a message of God's great love and gladness. In verse 25, we read:

> For David says concerning Him: "I foresaw the Lord always before my face, for He is at my right hand, that I may not be shaken. Therefore my heart rejoiced, and my tongue was glad; moreover my flesh also will rest in hope."

The gladness with which Jesus responds is not fleeting. Psalm 45:7 tells us, "Therefore God, Your God, has anointed You [the Messiah] with the oil of gladness more than Your companions." As He walked on earth—fully God and totally man—Jesus had been bathed in His Father's joy and gladness.

Zephaniah 3:17 also says that the Father rejoices over His creation with singing. Why? Because we are His kids; He loves us. Can you grasp that, rejoice in, take pleasure in the fact that the God of the universe sings to you of His love? He treasures you; you are the center of happiness and jubilation for the Father. He loves us with an unending love and celebrates us in song.

Rev. John Piper wrote of God's gladness:

> When I think of the voice of God singing, I hear the booming of Niagara Falls mingled with the trickle of a mossy mountain stream. I hear the blast of Mt. St. Helens mingled with a kitten's purr. I hear the power of an East Coast hurricane and the barely audible puff of a night snow in the woods. And I hear the unimaginable roar of the sun 865,000 miles thick, one million three hundred thousand times bigger than the earth, and nothing but fire, 1,000,000 degrees centigrade, on the cooler surface of the corona. But I hear this unimaginable roar mingled with the tender, warm crackling of the living room logs on a cozy winter's night.
>
> And when I hear this singing I stand dumbfounded, staggered, speechless that he is singing over me. He is rejoicing over my good with all his heart and with all his soul.[18]

It is impossible to be the heirs of such a great love and be unchanged. God desires that we share His gladness with those around us. How can we do that? We can practice obedience, radiate His love, and share His story of grace with others. God is not staring down at us with a big stick in hand waiting to punish us for our failures; no, He is leaning over the balcony of heaven singing a love song to His favored children.

—DISCUSSION—
MATERIAL

1. Read Psalm 16.

2. What do you think God sings about His children?

3. Write down four lines of His song.

4. What are the five points found in Zephaniah 3:17?

5. Name some of the Believer's benefits.

6. Read Psalm 122:1.

7. Is your response to worship one of gladness?

8. How can we prepare ourselves for worship?

9. Listen closely; can you hear God's song of gladness as He sings over you?

— SCRIPTURES ON —
GOD'S GLADNESS

Also in the day of your gladness, and in your solemn days, and in the beginnings of your months, ye shall blow with the trumpets over your burnt offerings, and over the sacrifices of your peace offerings; that they may be to you for a memorial before your God: I am the LORD your God.
NUMBERS 10:10 KJV

Because thou servedst not the LORD thy God with joyfulness, and with gladness of heart, for the abundance of all things.
DEUTERONOMY 28:47 KJV

Glory and honour are in his presence; strength and gladness are in his place.
1 CHRONICLES 16:27 KJV

Thou hast put gladness in my heart, more than in the time that their corn and their wine increased.
PSALM 4:7 KJV

Thou hast turned for me my mourning into dancing: thou hast put off my sackcloth, and girded me with gladness.
PSALM 30:11 KJV

Thou lovest righteousness, and hatest wickedness: therefore God, thy God, hath anointed thee with the oil of gladness above thy fellows.
PSALM 45:7 KJV

Light is sown for the righteous, and gladness for the upright in heart.
PSALM 97:11 KJV

Serve the LORD with gladness: come before his presence with singing.
PSALM 100:2 KJV

And he brought forth his people with joy, and his chosen with gladness.
PSALM 105:43 KJV

That I may see the good of thy chosen, that I may rejoice in the gladness of thy nation, that I may glory with thine inheritance.
PSALM 106:5,KJV

The hope of the righteous shall be gladness.
PROVERBS 10:28 KJV

CHAPTER SIX

GOD'S DELIVERANCE

Surely He shall deliver you from the snare of the fowler
[one who traps birds] and from the perilous pestilence.

PSALM 91:3

Had I tried to orchestrate my own life I would never have thought
to include some of the events in which I've had a role, major or
minor. Being involved in any aspect of the Iran–Contra Affair—
no way! And yet one day in March 1989 God's plan took me to
Washington, D.C. I had flown there at the rather secretive request
of Carolyn Sundseth, a friend who had served as religious liaison
in Ronald Reagan's administration.

"Mike, would you fly here to Washington tomorrow? I know
a man here who needs prayer. Don't ask his name, his position, or
why he needs prayer; just pray with him." I quickly agreed to make
the trek from Dallas to the capital, although I was puzzled as to
why she had called me. There were many other Bible-believing men
much closer to the White House.

Carolyn was waiting for me when I arrived at 1600 Pennsylvania
Avenue. As we walked down a hallway lined with a bank of windows, she pointed out a solitary young man staring pensively at the

landscape outside. "That's him," she whispered. "Just give him whatever word you feel God has given you."

The man, dressed in the full military uniform of a marine colonel, turned at the sound of my footfalls behind him. Suddenly, my mind was flooded with the portion of scripture I had read earlier that day. I reached my hand out to him. "Sir, you don't know me, but I have a message for you. God wants you to hear His Word:

> But now, thus says the Lord, who created you, O Jacob, And He who formed you, O Israel: "Fear not, for I have redeemed you; I have called you by your name; You are Mine. When you pass through the waters, I will be with you; And through the rivers, they shall not overflow you. When you walk through the fire, you shall not be burned, nor shall the flame scorch you" (Isaiah 43:1–2).

The man to whom God had just promised deliverance looked at me and nodded with only the hint of a bemused smile. He looked as though he was intimately acquainted with the fire of adversity. Neither of us spoke another word. We simply turned and went our separate ways. It would not be until sometime later that I would learn my White House encounter was with none other than Colonel Oliver North, who at the time was embroiled in the Iran–Contra Affair.

Having favor with God brings His deliverance. That is a word we don't often hear about in this day of "I can do it myself! I don't need God or anyone else." We may hear it used in a sermon about Moses leading the Hebrew children out of Egypt, and what an illustration that is—a nation within a nation badly in need of God's deliverance.

Yet there are people in our town, on our street, on our block who need God's deliverance.

Had Moses written Psalm 91, he might have thought of the "fowler" as the pharaohs, kings who had entrapped the children of Israel for four hundred years! David may have interpreted the "fowler" as King Saul, who tried so diligently to ensnare and kill him. In 1 Samuel 26:20 (NLT) David questions his predicament: "Why has the king of Israel come out to search for a single flea? Why does he hunt me down like a partridge on the mountains?" The Believer, however, knows that the fowler is a type of the Enemy of the soul, whose very existence is one of lies and betrayal, of enticement and entrapment. We need a Deliverer!

Four hundred years is a long time to wait for deliverance. Perhaps the Hebrew children had become disheartened, cynical, and despaired of ever again experiencing favor with the God of Abraham, Isaac, and Jacob. Then God raised up a man, Moses; called him from the backside of the desert; empowered him to lead His people out of Egypt into a land that God had promised. Early in his life, Moses had tried to take matters into his own hands only to be charged with murdering an Egyptian and finding himself a fugitive from justice. He fell into the snare of the fowler by thinking he had the answer without the benefit of God's instruction. His one-Egyptian-at-a-time campaign was far from what God wanted for him—or for His children. God's response to Moses' intervention was a forty-year sentence to life amidst the desert sands.

So Moses got comfortable: He took a wife, had children, shepherded a herd of stinky sheep, and forgot about Egypt. But God had other plans that involved a burning bush, a staff that became a snake, and returning home to face his past mistakes. Even with God's intervention, Moses balked at what was asked of him in Exodus 3:7–12 (NLT):

Then the LORD told him, "I have certainly seen the oppression of my people in Egypt. I have heard their cries of distress because of their harsh slave drivers. Yes, I am aware of their suffering. So I have come down to rescue them from the power of the Egyptians and lead them out of Egypt into their own fertile and spacious land. It is a land flowing with milk and honey—the land where the Canaanites, Hittites, Amorites, Perizzites, Hivites, and Jebusites now live. Look! The cry of the people of Israel has reached me, and I have seen how harshly the Egyptians abuse them. Now go, for I am sending you to Pharaoh. You must lead my people Israel out of Egypt." But Moses protested to God, "Who am I to appear before Pharaoh? Who am I to lead the people of Israel out of Egypt?" God answered, "I will be with you. And this is your sign that I am the one who has sent you: When you have brought the people out of Egypt, you will worship God at this very mountain."

Moses went to work straightaway trying to talk God into changing His mind. He offered one excuse after another, but Jehovah persisted. Moses wasn't the first to try to bow out—Gideon asked for one fleece after another to try to convince himself that God wasn't calling him to action; Jonah ran headlong into a storm and ended up in the belly of a big fish. And yet in the end each found favor with God and, under His direction, completed the task He had set before them. Each discovered that "when I am weak, then I am strong" (2 Corinthians 12:10).

God does not assign tasks and then walk away from us. No, His Word says, "I will go before you and make the crooked places straight" (Isaiah 45:2). Jehovah doesn't look for the man or woman who can get it done alone. The apostle Paul wrote in 1 Corinthians 1:18–19; 27:

> For the message of the cross is foolishness to those who are perishing, but to us who are being saved it is the power of God. For it is written: "I will destroy the wisdom of the wise, and bring to nothing the understanding of the prudent."...But God has chosen the foolish things of the world to put to shame the wise, and God has chosen the weak things of the world to put to shame the things which are mighty.

When Moses made the trek across the wilderness back to Egypt to deliver the children of Israel, he went with God's favor but not without challenges. God didn't promise an event-free journey. In fact, things got a lot worse for him before he reached Goshen.

Moses, his wife, Zipporah, and their two sons set out to cross the desert, and after a hard day's travel stopped for the night. It was there that he was again challenged by Jehovah to prove his obedience to the Abrahamic covenant upon penalty of death. This man God had called to deliver His people would soon learn that he could not fulfill his mission unless the covenant set forth in Genesis 17:10–11 had been honored:

This is My covenant which you shall keep, between Me and you and your descendants after you: Every male child among you shall be circumcised; and you shall be circumcised in the flesh of your foreskins, and it shall be a sign of the covenant between Me and you.

Moses and his sons were not exempt. As the adopted son of Pharaoh's daughter, he would not have undergone the Hebrew ritual of circumcision, as had every other son of Israel.

As God confronted Moses, Zipporah realized that her husband would die if she did not take action to save him. In a moment of desperation, she grabbed a flint knife and circumcised her son. Professor of Religion Dr. Steve Rodeheaver interprets this act:

Scripture says that she [Zipporah] then takes their son's foreskin and touches Moses' feet with it. "Feet" is a Hebrew euphemism for "private parts" (our own English euphemism for genitals). The genitals are so private that they are not mentioned. Every Israelite reading/hearing the story would know that Zipporah did not touch Moses' "feet" with the foreskin, but his private parts. In this way she performed a vicarious circumcision, identifying Moses with the circumcision of their son. Upon this act the LORD "let him alone" (4:26) and let Moses live. Zipporah's quick thinking (and cutting) saved Moses' life. (As a side note, notice that Moses has now been saved by four women: his mother, [his] sister, Pharaoh's daughter, and now his wife.)[19]

It was at that point Moses sent Zipporah and their sons back home to her father, Jethro, and made his way to Egypt to deliver God's message and His people. After Moses confronted Pharaoh, things got a lot worse for God's people. The Egyptian overseers made life miserable for them—doubling their daily quota of brick-making and beating them for the smallest infraction. As if that weren't enough, many of the Israelites adopted the ungodly worship of deities carved from wood or stone. The Egyptians suffered the devastating effects of a series of plagues that God poured out on the land, culminating in the Israelites being thrust out of Egypt.

God wanted the Egyptians—and the Israelites—to know that HE was the one who had orchestrated their release. He wanted no one else to be able to claim the honor:

> Then the LORD said to Moses, "Now you shall see what *I will do* to Pharaoh. For with a strong hand he will let them go, and with a strong hand he will drive them out of his land" (Exodus 6:1, emphasis mine).

Finally, Pharaoh caved in and allowed the Israelites to depart. It wasn't long before he realized he had just released his entire workforce—his slave labor. He called for the commanders of the army to bring them all back. Suddenly, the Hebrew children realized exactly where they were—caught between the devil and the deep blue sea—actually, they were between the armies of Pharaoh and the Red Sea. But Moses had favor with Jehovah. My picture of events is, perhaps, colored by the movie *The Ten Commandments*, with Charlton Heston as Moses. I picture him standing on a promontory near the sea with outstretched arms, reassuring the multitude following him. "Do not be afraid. Stand firm and you will see the deliverance the LORD will bring you today. The Egyptians you see today you will never see again" (Exodus 14:13 NIV).

If God had made all of this easy, there would have been no need to recognize or trust God. The goal was then, as it is now, to help us realize that Jehovah's intervention is vital; that without Him, they—and we—can do nothing (see John 15:5). But with Him all things are possible to him who believes (see Mark 9:23), even providing a path of dry ground through the midst of a roiling sea of adversity.

God is a God of deliverance. His redemptive plan is to save and deliver. Luke 4:18 is a microcosm of the purpose of Jesus on earth. He had gone to Nazareth, and the chapter tells us that it was His custom to go to the synagogue. Once there, the Torah scroll was presented to Jesus, and He began to read from the prophet Isaiah:

> The Spirit of the Lord *is* upon me, because he
> hath anointed me to preach the gospel to the poor;
> he hath sent me to heal the brokenhearted, to preach
> deliverance to the captives, and recovering of sight
> to the blind, to set at liberty them that are bruised
> (Luke 4:18 KJV).

Have you ever had to be delivered from a perilous situation? All of mankind was in a perilous situation when God sent His Son to deliver us from the wages of sin—death—and to provide the gift of eternal life. One of the great messages within the pages of Scripture is that of deliverance—Noah was delivered from the flood; Isaac was delivered from becoming a sacrifice because God provided a ram; Esther and her people were delivered from the wicked Haman; Daniel was delivered from the lions' den, and his friends—Shadrach, Meshach, and Abednego—were rescued from the fiery furnace; Jonah was delivered from the belly of the big fish; and David was delivered from the giant, Goliath. Each had been dramatically rescued from a desperate situation by Jehovah-Mephalti—God, my Deliverer!

Certainly as this book is being written, the Jewish people are in need of deliverance, and I thank God for protecting and delivering my son, Michael, in early August 2014. It was then that he emailed me the following:

> Today while on a fact-finding trip to the front line of the conflict between Israel and Hamas, we had a very close call: A mortar fired by Hamas narrowly missed our vehicle. Most of the time mortar fire is too small to set off the early warning system, so we had no idea it was coming. A short distance down the road the mortar struck and exploded. It is likely I would have been hit had we not stopped to minister to a group of Israeli soldiers in an open field. I left the area feeling that God had delivered me today.

Jehovah's deliverance is not just an element of Old Testament stories; it is as real today as it was then. We look again to the apostle Paul, who wrote in Colossians 1:13:

> He [God] has delivered us from the power of darkness and conveyed *us* into the kingdom of the Son of His love...

In Psalm 68:20, the psalmist penned:

God is to us a God of deliverance. To the LORD, the
Lord, belongs escape from death (HNV.)

And again in Psalm 144:1–2:

Blessed be the LORD my Rock, who trains my
hands for war, and my fingers for battle—my lovingkindness and my fortress, my high tower and my
deliverer, my shield and the One in whom I take refuge, who subdues my people under me.

There was another man written about in the Old Testament
who knew firsthand of God's power to deliver—and especially from
death. The man was Naaman. He was a mighty warrior, a commander in the army of the king of Aram (Syria), a country at war
with Israel. The Arameans had no knowledge of Jehovah, for they
were worshippers of Rimmon (Baal)—a wicked, bloodthirsty god
of a depraved and vicious people. They were the terrorists of their
day—a nation with no regard for the sanctity of human life. The
source of their coveted victory over Israel, or so they erroneously
thought, would be their god and their king, Ben Hadad. Naaman
was his closest advisor—a brilliant soldier. But he had a devastating
secret—one that would end not only his career, but eventually
threaten his life. What he didn't realize was that in the arsenal of
souvenirs he had claimed from sorties into Israel, there was a secret
weapon: a little slave girl that Naaman had brought home to serve
his wife. She was on the bottom rung of the social ladder; no human
rights, no safeguards, no redress. She possessed the one thing that
Naaman did not—freedom in the midst of captivity.

Naaman's deep, dark secret: he was a leper. Once discovered, he began his trek to one doctor after another, one sorcerer after another, one fortune-teller after another, all to no avail. Time and again, his condition was pronounced hopeless. No one had a cure for what was then an ultimately fatal disease. The great man would slowly waste away, bit by bit, until his life was gone.

But God had planted a witness in Naaman's household—the little slave girl. We are not told her name or her age, only of her compassionate nature toward her captor. One day she quietly approached her mistress with news she was sure would be welcomed:

> Then she said to her mistress, "If only my master were with the prophet who is in Samaria! For he would heal him of his leprosy" (2 Kings 5:3).

She boldly declared that the God of Elisha could deliver her master from the awful disease that had enveloped his body even though he was an enemy to Israel. This young missionary planted a seed that would soon grow to fruition. As Naaman listened to his wife recount the conversation, a spark began to ignite inside him; hope began to arise as he prepared to make a foray into the land of Israel—not to wage war against its people, but to battle his illness. He loaded a string of camels with the equivalent of $1 million in silver, gold, and goods. In his pouch, he tucked a letter of introduction from King Ben Hadad to the king of Israel; a letter that read (verse 6):

> Now be advised, when this letter comes to you, that I have sent Naaman my servant to you, that you may heal him of his leprosy.

Naaman was prepared: He had the funds, the letter of introduction, and the reputation. All he needed was for the king of Israel to wave a hand and pronounce him healed; but God had another plan. An old quotation often attributed to early church canon Thomas à Kempis says, "Man proposes; God disposes." Upon receipt of the letter, the king of Israel was consumed by fear, certain he was being set up for failure by Ben Hadad. He panicked:

> And it happened, when the king of Israel read the letter, that he tore his clothes and said, "Am I God, to kill and make alive, that this man sends a man to me to heal him of his leprosy? Therefore please consider, and see how he seeks a quarrel with me." So it was, when Elisha the man of God heard that the king of Israel had torn his clothes, that he sent to the king, saying, "Why have you torn your clothes? Please let him come to me, and he shall know that there is a prophet in Israel" (vv. 7–8).

So the proud soldier set off in search of the prophet in Israel. Surrounded by troops guarding the vast wealth Naaman had taken with him to Samaria, as well as horses, servants, and camels, he made his way to the house of Elisha and announced his presence. He was ready once again to receive deliverance from the terrors and ultimate death of leprosy. Naaman, whose pride stood between him and God, still had no clue that his vast wealth could never buy the blessings or deliverance of Jehovah-Rophe—the Lord our Healer. He could not know that God's deliverance is free of charge, that all He wants are "a broken spirit, a broken and a contrite heart" (see Psalm 51:17).

Sitting astride his magnificent mount, the commander waited for the prophet to show his face—probably becoming more and more irritated by the delay. Suddenly a man appeared; not the prophet himself, but his servant with a message: "Go and wash in the Jordan seven times, and your flesh shall be restored to you, and you shall be clean" (v. 10).

Naaman was livid! How dare this lowly prophet from nowhere send a servant to tell him to wash himself in the vile, muddy Jordan River! Why, he could return home and bathe in the pristine waters of one of the rivers of Damascus. He was done with this charlatan! He would pick up his marbles and go home! Little did he realize that healing was in his grasp—but only through the power of Jehovah and only by his obedience to the instructions of the prophet. God had no regard for Naaman's pride, position, possessions, or propositions. He simply wanted Naaman to abandon himself to the strong arms of a loving God and submit to His directive: Go and wash. The healing properties were not to be found in the waters of the Jordan, but in the obedience of Naaman.

Finally, one of his servants approached and entreated him:

> My father, if the prophet had told you to do something great, would you not have done it? How much more then, when he says to you, "Wash, and be clean"? (v. 13).

As he began to dip in the waters of the Jordan—once, twice, three times, four, five, six, and then seven times—humility and obedience brought favor with God and deliverance from the disease that had attacked his body:

So he went down and dipped seven times in the Jordan, according to the saying of the man of God; and his flesh was restored like the flesh of a little child, and he was clean (v. 14).

Understanding dawned as Naaman began to realize "Indeed, now I know that there is no God in all the earth, except in Israel; now therefore, please take a gift from your servant." God had promised deliverance. His command, I am certain, must have seemed irrational and totally impossible to the man from Damascus. But God's ways are far above man's ways! In his first letter to the Corinthians, the apostle Paul wrote:

But God has chosen the foolish things of the world to put to shame the wise, and God has chosen the weak things of the world to put to shame the things which are mighty; and the base things of the world and the things which are despised God has chosen, and the things which are not, to bring to nothing the things that are, that no flesh should glory in His presence (1 Corinthians 1:27–29).

Namaan returned home a changed man, healed and whole, professing his allegiance to the God of Israel.

This story is special to me. In the early 2000s I had written three books and, despite all my efforts, could not find a publisher. The royalties from those books would have added much-needed funds to ministry coffers to help pay bills. The books were: *God Wrestling, The Prayer of David: In Times of Trouble*, and *The Unanswered Prayers of Jesus* (based on John 17 and my own unanswered prayers).

The Holy Spirit prompted me to write yet another book. I reminded God that there were three unpublished manuscripts languishing on a shelf in my office—as if He didn't know that. The Spirit of the Lord replied, "I told Naaman to dip seven times. If I tell you to write seven books—published or not—obey My voice."

"Yes, Lord," I replied and in six days wrote *Beyond Iraq: The Next Move.*

When I had the published book in my hand, I called my daughter Rachel and asked her if she would go to New York City with me to promote the book. She accepted, and the next morning we boarded a flight. As soon as we checked in to our hotel, we each took a stack of books and began to make the rounds of the various television studios. Convinced that if God didn't open doors, I would sink, I was standing either on the brink of a disaster or a huge miracle.

On Sunday, Rachel and I attended Times Square Church, where my old friend David Wilkerson pastored. After the service, he graciously agreed to pray with me about the launch of the book. Although I appreciated his prayer, when we left the church I was unsure whether to stay in New York or go back to the hotel and pack my bags for home. We decided to stay one more night.

The next morning my phone rang. I was stunned when the voice on the other end identified herself as a producer for Neil Cavuto on the Fox News Channel. That was only the beginning. Over the next several months, I scheduled appearances on sixty-one programs— television and radio. By June, *Beyond Iraq* had sold 53,000 copies, and in July it hit the *New York Times* Best Sellers list in the top ten. That year, the publisher had a booth for *Beyond Iraq* at the Christian Booksellers Association Convention. When we walked toward the book-signing table, a line of people snaked down the corridor. My agent informed me that they were waiting for copies of my book.

It was the opening of a floodgate of books for me. In 2003 alone, I released *God Wrestling, The Unanswered Prayers of Jesus,* and *The Prayer of David.* Why? Because I was wrestling with God; I had unanswered prayers, and my middle name was David. I spent sixty-one days in prayer and fasting one meal a day before the windows of heaven were opened and the Word of God was again activated. There has been a steady stream of books since that time, as I have been blessed by favor with God.

In the second chapter of Joshua we are told of another divine intervention and miraculous deliverance; it is the story of Rahab, a prostitute. For seven long days, the children of Israel had gathered outside the walls of Jericho according to Jehovah's specific directions. Days before the march around the walls began, Joshua had sent two men to assess the situation inside the city. As they stealthily slipped from shadow to shadow down the streets, an alarm was given and the men were forced to run for their lives. They took refuge in the home of Rahab. Taking them up to the roof of the house, she hid them among stalks of flax that had been drying in the hot desert sun. Before covering them, she said to the men:

> I know that the LORD has given you the land, that the terror of you has fallen on us, and that all the inhabitants of the land are fainthearted because of you. For we have heard how the LORD dried up the water of the Red Sea for you when you came out of Egypt, and what you did to the two kings of the Amorites who were on the other side of the Jordan, Sihon and Og, whom you utterly destroyed. And as soon as we heard these things, our hearts melted;

neither did there remain any more courage in anyone because of you, for the LORD your God, He is God in heaven above and on earth beneath. Now therefore, I beg you, swear to me by the LORD, since I have shown you kindness, that you also will show kindness to my father's house, and give me a true token, and spare my father, my mother, my brothers, my sisters, and all that they have, and deliver our lives from death (Joshua 2:8–13).

The inhabitants of Jericho were moon worshippers, and the city a center for worship of that celestial body. They also worshipped the Canaanite god Molech and sacrificed their children by fire to appease the deity. With the advance of the children of Israel, God's judgment was about to fall on the people of that godless city—with one exception: the family of Rahab.

The lookouts posted on the wall could see the vast army of the Israelites as it approached the city, whose inner protective wall was said to have been approximately forty-five feet tall and twelve feet thick. The might of the advancing throng was well-known due to the defeat of the two Amorite kings—Og and Sihon—and the capture of their lands (see Numbers 21). Now this seemingly indestructible hoard approached Jericho, and the people were terrified—that is, until the marching began. Then the people inside the walls began to ridicule the Israelites.

One family inside the walls waited, however, not for Jehovah's destruction, but for His deliverance. After having saved the Israelite spies from the king's men who sought them, Rahab was given instruction for the salvation of her family:

So the men said to her: "We will be blameless of this oath of yours which you have made us swear, unless, when we come into the land, you bind this line of scarlet cord in the window through which you let us down, and unless you bring your father, your mother, your brothers, and all your father's household to your own home. So it shall be that whoever goes outside the doors of your house into the street, his blood shall be on his own head, and we will be guiltless. And whoever is with you in the house, his blood shall be on our head if a hand is laid on him. And if you tell this business of ours, then we will be free from your oath which you made us swear." Then she said, "According to your words, so be it." And she sent them away, and they departed. And she bound the scarlet cord in the window (vv.17–21).

Rahab didn't ponder the instructions; she didn't argue the pros and cons of what she had been told to do. She simply lowered the red cord from the window of her family's dwelling. Why did God choose a prostitute of all the people in Jericho? In Hebrews 11:31, we read, "By faith the harlot Rahab did not perish with those who did not believe, when she had received the spies with peace." She and her family were delivered because of her faith and obedience. That is supported by her response in Joshua chapter 2. She, along with the other inhabitants, had heard of the exploits of the God of Israel. They responded with fear; she responded with faith. Then she took steps to exhibit her confidence in Jehovah: She followed their instructions and met the conditions outlined by the two spies:

✧ A red cord hung from her window;

✧ Her entire family was gathered as had been instructed;

✧ She kept silent, not divulging what she had learned from the two Israelites.

After seven days of marching in complete silence, the priests blew the ram's horns and the "wall fell down flat" (see Joshua 6:20). The story continues:

> But Joshua had said to the two men who had spied out the country, "Go into the harlot's house, and from there bring out the woman and all that she has, as you swore to her." And the young men who had been spies went in and brought out Rahab, her father, her mother, her brothers, and all that she had. So they brought out all her relatives and left them outside the camp of Israel. But they burned the city and all that was in it with fire. Only the silver and gold, and the vessels of bronze and iron, they put into the treasury of the house of the LORD. And Joshua spared Rahab the harlot, her father's household, and all that she had (Joshua 6:22–25).

According to authors C. F. Keil and Franz Delitzsch:

> But the Lord so guided the course of the spies, that they found in this sinner the very person who

was the most suitable for their purpose, and upon whose heart the tidings of the miracles wrought by the living God on behalf of Israel had made such an impression, that she not only informed the spies of the despondency of the Canaanites, but, with believing trust in the power of the God of Israel, concealed the spies from all the inquiries of her countrymen, though at the greatest risk to herself.[20]

In Matthew 1:5–6, we can trace the lineage of the harlot who was delivered by the power of God: Salmon begot Boaz by Rahab, Boaz begot Obed by Ruth, Obed begot Jesse, and Jesse begot David the king.

Quite simply, deliverance means turning from unrighteousness to righteousness—making a 180-degree turn from sin to salvation. It is then and only then that, like Naaman and Rahab and countless others, we can find deliverance and favor with God.

— DISCUSSION —
MATERIAL

1. Read 2 Kings 5.

2. Have you ever felt as if you were caught in the "snare of the fowler"?

3. What do you think of when you hear the word *deliverance*?

4. Does God expect us to accomplish tasks alone?

5. Why do we so often try to do things in our own strength?

6. Can you recollect a time when waiting on the Lord provided the answer?

7. What was the one thing God required of Naaman above all else?

8. There were two non-Jews in the lineage of Christ. Rahab was one; who was the other? Why do you think they were included?

—SCRIPTURES ON—
GOD'S DELIVERANCE

The righteous cry, and the LORD heareth, and delivereth them out of all their troubles.
PSALM 34:17 KJV

Then they cried unto the LORD in their trouble, and he delivered them out of their distresses.
PSALM 107:6 KJV

And he said, The LORD is my rock, and my fortress, and my deliverer.
2 SAMUEL 22:2 KJV

The Lord knoweth how to deliver the godly out of temptations, and to reserve the unjust unto the day of judgment to be punished.
2 PETER 2:9 KJV

And David spake unto the LORD the words of this song in the day that the LORD had delivered him out of the hand of all his enemies, and out of the hand of Saul.
2 SAMUEL 22:1 KJV

I sought the LORD, and he heard me, and delivered me from all my fears.
PSALM 34:4 KJV

But I am poor and needy; yet the Lord thinketh upon me: thou art my help and my deliverer; make no tarrying, O my God.
PSALM 40:17 KJV

Be pleased, O LORD, to deliver me: O LORD, make haste to help me.
PSALM 40:13 KJV

Truly my soul finds rest in God; my salvation comes from him. Truly he is my rock and my salvation; he is my fortress, I will never be shaken. ... Yes, my soul, find rest in God; my hope comes from him. Truly he is my rock and my salvation; he is my fortress, I will not be shaken. My salvation and my honor depend on God; he is my mighty rock, my refuge. Trust in him at all times, you people; pour out your hearts to him, for God is our refuge.

PSALM 62:1–2, 5–8 NIV

CHAPTER SEVEN

GOD'S GRACE

The king loved Esther more than all the other women,
and she obtained grace and favor in his sight more
than all the virgins; so he set the royal crown upon
her head and made her queen instead of Vashti.

ESTHER 2:17

GOD'S GRACE AND UNMERITED FAVOR can be defined by three phrases: 1) love that does not compromise; 2) kindness that does not yield to outside pressure; and 3) strength that is revolutionary. God's grace and unyielding favor was never more evident to me than when I was in Geneva, Switzerland, in December 1988.

I had flown there to seek admittance to the United Nations General Assembly—another dark episode in the history of Israel. That tiny nation had again been dragged to the bargaining table in an attempt to achieve calm in the midst of its ravening enemies. Palestine Liberation Organization Chairman Yasser Arafat had been asked to denounce terrorism and acknowledge Israel's very right to existence. He did an exceedingly poor job of both and was forced to call a press conference to clarify his position. The incident was highly controlled by Arafat's executive council and was not to be readily available to the general public—meaning ordinary people like me.

When I heard rumors of this upcoming meeting, I began to walk the halls of the venue and to pray. After a time I felt led by the Spirit of God to go to room 401. Once I had gained access to the chamber, I walked to the second row of seats and placed my locked briefcase on the chair in the center of the row, and then left the area. Several hours later, PLO terrorists began to file into that room. It was filled to capacity when I approached one of the guards and requested that I be allowed to take my seat. He informed me brusquely that I had no seat in the room.

I asked him to look on the center chair in the second row; there he would find my locked briefcase with the combination: 0001. I advised him that my passport was inside the case. Reluctantly, he turned and stalked up the aisle. Shortly he came back and escorted me to the chair that held my briefcase. Minutes later, Arafat entered. The chair I had been led to select was directly in front of him. The camera crews had been assigned row three—just behind me. The cameramen were incensed because my head was in the way.

Before me was a table where Arafat and the few men who would accompany him were to sit. They entered the room, and the PLO chairman delivered his speech. Afterward, he said, "I shall allow three of you to speak. You may choose among yourselves."

Knowing I would not be chosen, I clutched my Bible, stood to my feet, and held aloft a copy of the PLO charter and shouted, "Mr. Arafat, if you denounce terrorism, then condemn this covenant that calls for the destruction of Israel." Raising my Bible in the other hand, I began to recount the biblical position of the Jewish people.

Arafat screamed: "Shut up, shut up! What must I do to make you shut up?" When he paused in his rant, I turned and was met by the hate-filled stares of PLO members in the room. I prayed, "Lord, you divided the sea for Moses; all I need is about a foot to get out of here." Suddenly, I was surrounded by God's grace and favor. It was as if a carpet had been rolled out, and before me was a path of escape. I walked quickly through the midst of a phalanx of terrorists into the dark hallway. As if led by an unseen usher, I found an exit, climbed into a taxi, and was taken back to the hotel. Once again, I had been the recipient of favor with God and His grace so freely given to the Believer.

Daily we enjoy the freely given—but not cheap—grace of God. It comes to us only by the shed blood of Jesus Christ. The noted German pastor Dietrich Bonhoeffer wrote:

> Cheap grace is preaching forgiveness without requiring repentance, baptism without church discipline, Communion without confession. ... Cheap grace is grace without discipleship, grace without the cross, grace without Jesus Christ, living and incarnate.[21]

Only when we as Believers comprehend all that grace is not, can we fully appreciate its splendor. Grace is a gift freely given, a pardon—not because of anything you and I have done, but because of God's love for His children. It is undeserved compassion, something that can never be earned through works. Favor with God is offered purely because of the kindness of the Giver.

Noted theologian J. I. Packer described grace this way:

> In the New Testament grace means God's love in action toward men who merited the opposite of love. Grace means God moving heaven and earth to save

sinners who could not lift a finger to save themselves. Grace means God sending His only Son to descend into hell on the cross so that we guilty ones might be reconciled to God and received into heaven.[22]

II Corinthians 5:21, NKJV, reads: For He made Him who knew no sin *to be* sin for us, that we might become the righteousness of God in Him.

In reflecting on the birth of Jesus, the apostle John recalled:

And the Word became flesh and dwelt among us, and we beheld His glory, the glory as of the only begotten of the Father, *full of grace and truth* (John 1:14, emphasis mine).

Jesus was different from any man who had ever walked the earth. He was, if you will, a revolutionary. He presented a gospel of grace radically different from the legalism the children of Israel had experienced under the Law of Moses. In verse 17, John goes on to say:

For the law was given through Moses, *but* grace and truth came through Jesus Christ.

Under the laws given to Moses in the Sinai, there were onerous burdens and exasperating rules and regulations. The Pharisees added even more stringent measures to increase the weight placed on the people. Neither grace nor joy had any role in the Mosaic Law; no wonder the teachings of Jesus were such a breath of fresh air. The Pharisees were obsessed with responsibility, outward behavior, and an unerring attention to right and wrong. Submissiveness was dictated by stern obligation, not a process ordained by love and grace.

In Luke 6:6–11, Jesus was in the synagogue on the Sabbath:

> Now it happened on another Sabbath, also, that He entered the synagogue and taught. And a man was there whose right hand was withered. So the scribes and Pharisees watched Him closely, whether He would heal on the Sabbath, that they might find an accusation against Him. But He knew their thoughts, and said to the man who had the withered hand, "Arise and stand here." And he arose and stood. Then Jesus said to them, "I will ask you one thing: Is it lawful on the Sabbath to do good or to do evil, to save life or to destroy?" And when He had looked around at them all, He said to the man, "Stretch out your hand." And he did so, and his hand was restored as whole as the other.

The scribes and Pharisees in attendance were thinking not of the diseased, disabled, or distressed, but of how they might lay a trap for Jesus. They walked headlong into a perfect opportunity when Jesus saw that man with a withered hand in the crowd. The religionists offered condemnation; Jesus offered grace. Of the accounts in the Gospels, Luke's is the only one revealing that it was the *right* hand that was shrunken and useless. Since the *left* hand was used to take care of all bodily functions, it was considered unclean. No Jew was to conduct business of any kind with the left hand—handshakes, blessings, even sharing a meal. With his emaciated right hand, the man in question was handicapped physically and mentally.

Verse 7 says the scribes and Pharisees "watched Him closely, whether He would heal on the Sabbath, that they might find an accusation against Him." No concern for the dilemma of the victim; not an inkling of compassion, just intense scrutiny for the sake of criticism.

The critics had no idea that Jesus was well aware of their thought process. Despite the palpable contempt emanating from His detractors, Jesus walked up to the man and said to him, "Arise and stand here." Then He queried His detractors if it was deemed proper to do good on the Sabbath and to save a life. Today He might have asked, "Do I extend grace and healing, or do I walk away and let him continue to suffer the indignity of his problem?"

Hearing no response, Jesus told the man to stretch out his hand and it was fully restored! Did the scribes and Pharisees rejoice? Hardly! They were furious, giving little thought to anything other than their foiled plot to discredit the Healer.

The people in the courtyard of the synagogue understood the Mosaic Law and its constraints: The Old Testament prophets reminded the Israelites of their sins; Christ offered righteousness through His blood. Jesus offered grace as an alternative to the legalistic nature of the law that He had come to fulfill. It is because of God's grace in the person of Jesus Christ on the cross that we can have eternal life.

Amazing grace, how sweet the sound to the ears of the condemned; what joy to you and me! There must have been those standing nearby who were waiting to see the Pharisees tear Jesus apart. Rev. John Sowers said of that moment:

> These words of Jesus are for each of us; they are
> words that free us from the soul-destroying powers

of the judgment of the Pharisees.... Jesus does not condemn us. He frees us from condemnation. He frees us just as much from our sin. The one without sin, who alone could condemn, alone bore our sin and condemnation on the cross. His death frees us and his resurrection gives us a life that can be lived without the death and trap of sin.[23]

Grace is not an excuse to sin. The apostle Paul addressed that in his letter to the Romans:

> What then? Shall we sin because we are not under law but under grace? Certainly not! (Romans 6:15)

As Pastor Robert L. (Bob) Deffinbaugh so eloquently said:

> "While sin is an occasion for grace, grace is never to be an occasion for sin."[24]

Baptist preacher Charles Spurgeon asked the question: "If grace does not make you to differ from your own surroundings, is it really grace at all?"[25] When the woman caught in adultery came face-to-face with Grace, she was set free from the destructive judgment of the Pharisees and from the consequences of her sin. "Neither do I condemn thee!" said our Savior. She was set free to live a life of grace and favor with God, free to "go and sin no more."

Grace is God's character; it is as inherently a part of Him as is His love. It is evidenced in the Old Testament—in the lives of Jonah, David, Noah, and others, but it was fully demonstrated in the life of His Son, Jesus. It is because of His unlimited grace that you and

I have redemption, our sins forgiven, and a home awaiting us in heaven. As the apostle Paul wrote in Titus 2:11:

> For the grace of God that brings salvation has appeared to all men.

Perhaps the greatest expression of grace can be found on Golgotha, that lonely and bloody hill on the outskirts of Jerusalem. It is there that grace kissed the earth as God's plan of redemption unfolded. It is the silver cord that links the past and present to all eternity. It is the bridge that spans the great divide between earth and heaven. It is the covering that wraps the gift of justification—the declaration that you and I have been pronounced "Not guilty." In his letter to the Ephesians, chapter 2, Paul wrote:

> For by grace you have been saved through faith, and that not of yourselves; it is the gift of God, not of works, lest anyone should boast.

Author and Pastor Max Lucado wrote of grace:

> The wages of sin is death. Heaven's justice demands a death for your sin. Heaven's love, however, can't bear to see you die. So here is what God did. He stood and removed his heavenly robes. He came to earth to tell us that he would die for us. He would be our Savior. And that is what he did.[26]
>
> Grace is God's sudden, calming presence during the stormy seas of our lives. We hear his voice; we take the step.

Why? Because we are great sinners and we need a great Savior.... And surprisingly, we are able to walk on water. Death is disarmed. Failures are forgivable. Life has real purpose. And God is not only within sight, he is within reach.[27]

The apostle Paul assured the Romans in chapter 5, verse 20 that "where sin abounded, grace abounded much more."

In his book *The Grace Awakening*, Charles Swindoll wrote:

Yes, I know there will be times when we may momentarily fail, but they will be the exceptions rather than the rule of our day. We are under new ownership. Prompted by love, we serve a new master, Christ, not the old one who mistreated us. There is something exciting about enjoying a relationship with our new Friend.[28]

There are four things we must never forget about grace:

- ✦ It is independent of our works. We cannot work our way into heaven.

- ✦ It is undeserved. Nothing you or I can do will ever merit God's grace.

- ✦ It is inflexible. Grace remains static whether we pray every morning, or forget in our rush to get out the door.

- ✦ It is endless, eternal.

In this "pull yourself up by your own bootstraps" society in which we live, it is difficult to grasp the understanding that a life filled with God's grace is indicated by liberty, not by slavery; by gladness, not apathy; by happiness, not fear. Our responsibility is not canceled by grace—whether it is reading the Bible, prayer, or serving others; it is simply the oil that keeps friction at bay and reminds us constantly of God's love for His children.

It is all too easy to allow our lives to become dominated by fear that we have failed God or fallen short of His expectations; to believe that we have broken covenant with the Father. That is a lie whispered to us by the Father of Lies, Satan. He wants us to miss the point that Jesus is the bridge between us and Jehovah. It is He who has fulfilled the law and offered us His abundant and all-sufficient grace that falls on us from above.

As beloved children of God, surrounded by His grace, we have favor with Him. The most joyful people in the world are those who surrender daily and allow God's grace to govern their lives.

—DISCUSSION—
MATERIAL

1. What is grace?

2. Why is it so important in the life of the Believer?

3. What is the difference between legalism and grace?

4. Why did the Pharisees try so often to entrap Jesus?

5. Can you answer Spurgeon's question: If grace does not make you to differ from your own surroundings, is it really grace at all?

6. What four things must we never forget about grace?

7. How does the reality of God's grace calm our fears?

— SCRIPTURES ON —
GOD'S GRACE

And he said unto me, My grace is sufficient for thee: for my strength is made perfect in weakness. Most gladly therefore will I rather glory in my infirmities, that the power of Christ may rest upon me.

2 CORINTHIANS 12:9–12, KJV

But none of these things move me, neither count I my life dear unto myself, so that I might finish my course with joy, and the ministry, which I have received of the Lord Jesus, to testify the gospel of the grace of God.

ACTS 20:24 KJV

Let us therefore come boldly unto the throne of grace, that we may obtain mercy, and find grace to help in time of need.

HEBREWS 4:16 KJV

Thou therefore, my son, be strong in the grace that is in Christ Jesus.

2 TIMOTHY 2:1 KJV

For by grace are ye saved through faith; and that not of yourselves: it is the gift of God.

EPHESIANS 2:8 KJV

And if by grace, then is it no more of works: otherwise grace is no more grace. But if it be of works, then is it no more grace: otherwise work is no more work.

ROMANS 11:6 KJV

But Noah found grace in the eyes of the LORD.

GENESIS 6:8

You are fairer than the sons of men; grace is poured upon Your lips; therefore God has blessed You forever.

PSALM 45:2

And I will pour on the house of David and on the inhabitants of Jerusalem the Spirit of grace and supplication; then they will look on Me whom they pierced. Yes, they will mourn for Him as one mourns for his only son, and grieve for Him as one grieves for a firstborn.
ZECHARIAH 12:10

And the Child grew and became strong in spirit, filled with wisdom; and the grace of God was upon Him.
LUKE 2:40

And with great power the apostles gave witness to the resurrection of the Lord Jesus. And great grace was upon them all.
ACTS 4:33

For if by the one man's offense death reigned through the one, much more those who receive abundance of grace and of the gift of righteousness will reign in life through the One, Jesus Christ.
ROMANS 5:17

The grace of the Lord Jesus Christ, and the love of God, and the communion of the Holy Spirit be with you all. Amen.
2 CORINTHIANS 13:14

You have become estranged from Christ, you who attempt to be justified by law; you have fallen from grace.
GALATIANS 5:4

In Him we have redemption through His blood, the forgiveness of sins, according to the riches of His grace.
EPHESIANS 1:7

But to each one of us grace was given according to the measure of Christ's gift.
EPHESIANS 4:7

Therefore, since we are receiving a kingdom which cannot be shaken, let us have grace, by which we may serve God acceptably with reverence and godly fear.
HEBREWS 12:28

CHAPTER EIGHT

GOD'S PLEASURE IN HIS CHILDREN

For the LORD takes pleasure in His people; He will beautify the humble with salvation.

PSALM 149:4

AFTER I RETURNED FROM SOUTH KOREA and my stint of duty in the US Army, I was assigned to a recruiting post in Philadelphia. In the "City of Brotherly Love" I was robbed of all my belongings—clothes, wallet, and vehicle. The only place I could find to get off the streets was a bed at the Salvation Army. After several nights there, I received my army pay and was able to rent a room at a local YMCA. Night after night in my sparsely furnished room, I would close myself in with God, praying and searching the Scriptures, much as I had done in Korea. I drank only water that week as I beseeched God in prayer. I pointed to a battered chair in the corner and prayed, "Jesus, this is Your chair. Please come, sit and talk with me; I am ready to listen and obey." As I fasted and prayed, I read through the entire New Testament.

When I completed the New Testament, I picked up a book

called *The Cross and the Switchblade*. I was deeply moved by this book written by a preacher—David Wilkerson—who had reached out to drug addicts on the streets of New York. I began doing that in Philadelphia. Each day after work I would pass out Gospel tracts and share Jesus with people on the streets while I continued to seek God's plan for my life.

My first call to the ministry was as an evangelist, and it came not in my room at the YMCA but in a small, run-down restaurant on a Christmas morning. Sitting in a booth in the corner with my Bible open before me, I suddenly felt the presence of God envelop me. I bowed my head, and tears slipped silently down my face as I reveled in the warmth of the Holy Spirit. The word *evangelist* lodged in my thoughts. Doubts assailed me as I offered up a prayer of surrender: "Lord, I don't know what an evangelist does, but I know You are calling me to be one. I'm just garbage, but if You can use garbage, my life is Yours." At that point in my life, I had little understanding of the reality that God took great pleasure in me; that I was His beloved child, purchased at a great price and treasured.

As I sought God and began to worship Him and study His Word, it soon became apparent that every activity in which I participated could be turned into worship. As 1 Corinthians 10:31 reminds us, "Therefore, whether you eat or drink, or whatever you do, do all to the glory of God." That is the purpose of our lives—to bring pleasure and glory to God. Even German theologian Martin Luther knew our purpose: That no one was too small or great to achieve it, for he said, "A dairymaid can milk cows to the glory of God."[29]

As one acquaintance so succinctly paraphrased Ecclesiastes 9:10 ("Whatever your hand finds to do, do *it* with your might.") as "Whatever your hand finds to do, *do it right*." You and I need to do everything we do as unto our Lord, or as Colossians 3:23 (ESV) says:

Whatever you do, work heartily, as for the Lord
and not for men...

We adopt a lifestyle of worship that brings pleasure to our Lord.
For too long we have sought the pot of gold at the end of the
rainbow, the perfect marriage, or the world's idea of beauty. We have
failed to understand and recognize how precious and delightful we
are to the God of all Creation.

Author C. S. Lewis wrote:

> The problem of reconciling human suffering with
> the existence of a God who loves, is only insoluble so
> long as we attach a trivial meaning to the word "love",
> and look on things as if man were the centre of them.
> Man is not the centre. God does not exist for the sake
> of man. Man does not exist for his own sake. "Thou
> hast created all things, and for thy pleasure they are
> and were created." We were made not primarily that
> we may love God (though we were made for that too)
> but that God may love us, that we may become objects
> in which the Divine love may rest "well pleased".[30]

Genesis 1:31 says of the creation:

> Then God saw everything that He had made, and
> indeed *it was* very good.

The God of the universe formed Adam and Eve for the specific
function of pleasing Himself. He receives pleasure from you and
me. That is difficult to understand—especially for a man who, as a

child, suffered abuse and feelings of worthlessness at the hands of my earthly father. To realize that God takes pleasure in me is overwhelming.

Ephesians 1:5 reveals a great truth:

> God decided in advance to adopt us into his own family by bringing us to himself through Jesus Christ. This is what he wanted to do, *and it gave him great pleasure* (NLT, emphasis mine).

Your arrival on this planet gave God great pleasure. He was under no obligation to create mankind, but He chose to do so in order that we might have fellowship with Him. You and I have a distinct purpose: living to give pleasure to God. Could anything be more satisfying and rewarding?

How can we possibly bring pleasure to God? Psalm 147:11 provides an answer:

> The LORD takes pleasure in those who fear Him,
> in those who hope in His mercy.

God takes great delight in our worship, which is so much more than mere words or music; it is our very existence. It is everything we do and everything we say. It is reading the Word, praying, worshipping, sitting in silence before Him, or partaking of communion in remembrance of our Savior. Adam worshipped with his sacrifice in the garden of Eden; David worshipped with his harp and lyre on the hillsides of ancient Israel; Jesus bowed His body in worship and surrender in the garden of Gethsemane. Each was a very special moment dedicated to the One who takes pleasure in our sacrifice, our song, and our submission.

Christian psychologist David G. Meyers wrote in his book *The Pursuit of Happiness: Discovering the Pathway to Fulfillment, Well-Being, and Enduring Personal Joy*, of the nightmare that results in rushing headlong after this world's pleasures:

> Never has a culture experienced such comfort and opportunity, or such widespread depression.
>
> Never has a technology given us so many conveniences, or such terrible instruments of degradation and destruction.
>
> Never have we been so self-reliant, or so lonely...
>
> Never have we been so sophisticated about pleasure, or so likely to suffer broken or miserable marriages.[31]

How can we find our way out of the morass that Dr. Meyers portrays and bring pleasure to God? In his book *The Purpose Driven Life*, Pastor Rick Warren gives us the answer—it is through worship. He writes:

> Worship is not a *part* of your life; it *is* your life. Worship is not just for church services.... In the Bible people praised God at work, at home, in battle, in jail [remember Paul and Silas], and even in bed [Psalm 63:5–6]. Every activity can be transformed into an act of worship when you do it for the praise, glory, and pleasure of God.[32]

God desires that we worship Him totally—body, soul, mind, and spirit—all day, every day; from the rising of the sun to the going down of the same; His name is to be praised (see Psalm 113:3).

Dr. Sam Storms, an Oklahoma City pastor, offered this bit of insight into worship:

> If you come to worship for any reason other than the joy and pleasure and satisfaction that are to be found in God, you dishonor Him.... God's greatest delight is your delight in Him.[33]

In 1 Peter 2:9, the apostle wrote, "But you *are* a chosen generation, a royal priesthood, a holy nation, His own special people." My friend, you and I belong to God; we are special to Him; He takes pleasure in us. God created us to praise Him throughout all eternity—life without end. You were not an accident; you matter to God the Father. You were created in His image, for His purpose, in His time, and according to His plan and will.

John, the Revelator, wrote in chapter 4, verse 11, of Revelation (KJV):

> Thou art worthy, O Lord, to receive glory and honour and power: for thou hast created all things, and for thy pleasure they are and were created.

There lies the answer to the age-old question: Why was mankind created? The answer: "For thy pleasure."

In Psalm 104:31, we read: "May the glory of the LORD endure forever; May the LORD rejoice in His works." The entire psalm is one beautiful song about the beauty of God's creation. He rejoices over His creation—over you and me. His love overshadows us; His delight uplifts us; His song surrounds us. God rejoices in all that He has made; we are His handiwork. Noted theologian A. W. Tozer wrote:

> The Lord takes peculiar pleasure in His saints. Many think of God as far removed, gloomy and mightily displeased with everything, gazing down in a mood of fixed apathy upon a world in which He has long ago lost interest; but this is to think erroneously. True, God hates sin and can never look with pleasure upon iniquity, but where men seek to do God's will He responds in genuine affection. Christ in His atonement has removed the bar to the divine fellowship. Now in Christ all believing souls are objects of God's delight.[34]

That we were created for God's pleasure could possibly seem a bit strange—until we recognize the eternal truth that God is not egotistical; not one bit! He is totally selfless. When we focus on Self, we totally miss the purpose for which the Creator made us. We only find lasting joy when we focus on Him, for that is the reason for our existence—to honor, serve, and worship Jehovah-Bara—the Lord our Creator. He is holy; He is caring; and He is benevolent. The enigma of creation is that when we greedily pursue self-satisfaction, it is of no eternal value; but when we strive to delight our heavenly Father, we are laying up treasures for all eternity.

The Living Bible translation of Hosea 6:6 says, "I don't want your sacrifices—I want your love! I don't want your offerings—I want you to know me"! And He wants to shower us with His favor.

—DISCUSSION—
MATERIAL

1. Read Psalm 149.

2. Discuss the following: God takes pleasure in you.

3. What do His children do that brings God pleasure?

4. What is the purpose of praise and worship?

5. Is it just singing songs on Sunday?

6. How did some of the men and women in the Bible worship Jehovah?

7. Why was mankind created?

8. Read Psalm 104.

— SCRIPTURES ON —
GOD'S PLEASURE IN HIS CHILDREN

My voice You shall hear in the morning, O LORD; in the morning I will direct it to You, and I will look up. For You are not a God who takes pleasure in wickedness, nor shall evil dwell with You.

PSALM 5:3–4

Let them shout for joy and be glad, who favor my righteous cause; and let them say continually, "Let the LORD be magnified, who has pleasure in the prosperity of His servant."

PSALM 35:27

Bless the LORD, all you His hosts, You ministers of His, who do His pleasure. Bless the LORD, all His works, in all places of His dominion. Bless the LORD, O my soul!

PSALM 103:21–22

The LORD takes pleasure in those who fear Him, in those who hope in His mercy.

PSALM 147:11

For the LORD takes pleasure in His people; He will beautify the humble with salvation.

PSALM 149:4

Is this not the fast that I have chosen: To loose the bonds of wickedness, to undo the heavy burdens, to let the oppressed go free, and that you break every yoke? Is it not to share your bread with the hungry, and that you bring to your house the poor who are cast out; when you see the naked, that you cover him, and not hide yourself from your own flesh? Then your light shall break forth like the morning, your healing shall spring forth speedily, and your

righteousness shall go before you; the glory of the LORD shall be your rear guard. Then you shall call, and the LORD will answer; you shall cry, and He will say, "Here I am." If you take away the yoke from your midst, the pointing of the finger, and speaking wickedness, if you extend your soul to the hungry and satisfy the afflicted soul, then your light shall dawn in the darkness, and your darkness shall be as the noonday. The LORD will guide you continually, and satisfy your soul in drought, and strengthen your bones; you shall be like a watered garden, and like a spring of water, whose waters do not fail. Those from among you shall build the old waste places; you shall raise up the foundations of many generations; and you shall be called the Repairer of the Breach, the Restorer of Streets to Dwell In. If you turn away your foot from the Sabbath, from doing your pleasure on My holy day, and call the Sabbath a delight, the holy day of the LORD honorable, and shall honor Him, not doing your own ways, nor finding your own pleasure, nor speaking your own words, then you shall delight yourself in the LORD; and I will cause you to ride on the high hills of the earth, and feed you with the heritage of Jacob your father. The mouth of the LORD has spoken.
ISAIAH 58:6–14

Therefore, my beloved, as you have always obeyed, not as in my presence only, but now much more in my absence, work out your own salvation with fear and trembling; for it is God who works in you both to will and to do for His good pleasure.
PHILIPPIANS 2:12–13

Therefore we also pray always for you that our God would count you worthy of this calling, and fulfill all the good pleasure of His goodness and the work of faith with power, that the name of our Lord Jesus Christ may be glorified in you, and you in Him, according to the grace of our God and the Lord Jesus Christ.
2 THESSALONIANS 1:11–12

CHAPTER NINE

GOD'S FORGIVENESS

Judge not, and you shall not be judged. Condemn not, and you shall not be condemned. Forgive, and you will be forgiven.

LUKE 6:37

ONE SUNDAY MORNING A MAN whose name was Ray approached me after church and introduced himself. After we had chatted for a few minutes Ray, who seemed like a very godly man, said the Lord had impressed him to ask me for help. He needed to borrow $32,500 for one week. He offered to give me a post-dated check, which I was to deposit at a specified time. Not taking time to pray about it and wanting to help a brother in need, I agreed to his proposal. The next day Ray accompanied me to the bank, where I secured a cashier's check in the amount he needed, and in turn he handed me the post-dated check. Ray skipped town with our money and left me holding a worthless piece of paper.

I was devastated! Jesus kept admonishing me to "Forgive ... forgive." Finally I snapped, "Easy for You to say 'forgive'! He didn't rip off Your $32,500! It was mine! I've been saving for a long time; that's my kids' college fund." The moment I said that, I realized my ignorance. God had given His Son for me—and for Ray. Everything I had was His. I fell on my knees in my bedroom and prayed, "I forgive Ray, Lord. Help him to make things right with You."

I felt strongly that because I had forgiven Ray, our nest egg would be returned. A scripture in Proverbs flooded my spirit: "Yet when he [the thief] is found, he must restore sevenfold." That night I wrote the word *Return* on a piece of paper. As I held it up before God, I felt impressed to write a book titled *The Return*. Within ninety days the book was a reality and in the next twelve months became a bestseller. The royalty from sales was exactly seven times what had been stolen from us! And all because God had urged forgiveness.

Forgiveness! With His teachings on love, grace, and forgiveness, Jesus turned the old "eye for an eye" crowd on its collective head. His thanks for freeing them from that life of revenge were an arrest, a kangaroo-court conviction, a beating, mockery, and crucifixion. He had been marched through the streets of Jerusalem struggling to drag the cross of torture on His shoulders. Now He had collapsed on Golgotha, the hill of execution. The spikes and ropes were in place and the cross was raised against the sky. With a thud, it hurtled unimpeded into the hole that would hold it upright.

Some in the crowd looked upon Jesus—naked before the world, beaten to within an inch of His life, bruised and bloody—with satisfaction. Their purpose had been accomplished. I can easily imagine that Satan and all the demons in hell were dancing with glee. The Son of God was near death. The Enemy was certain he had won! Other bystanders bowed their heads in shame and compassion. Their beloved friend and companion hung exposed to the world. Tears rolled down those faces, and sobs could be heard echoing from the hill. As they watched in agony, the indifferent soldiers gathered in a circle at the foot of the cross. "Where are the dice?" one called. "Let's cast lots for His clothes."

As they began to gamble, a whisper issued from the mouth of Jesus and echoed through the halls of eternity. His first words spoken from the cross were "Father, forgive them, for they do not know what they are doing" (Luke 23:34 NIV).

Astonished, the soldiers must have momentarily halted their grisly game and looked heavenward. They were accustomed to hearing screams and curses, pleas of innocence, entreaties for mercy, appeals for water, but a prayer for forgiveness—unimaginable! The Man on the cross had prayed for them, pleading for God's forgiveness for their actions! The Son knew the Father in all of His mercy and His richly abounding love. He knew the words penned in Exodus:

> "The LORD, the LORD, the compassionate and gra-
> cious God, slow to anger, abounding in love and faith-
> fulness, maintaining love to thousands, and forgiving
> wickedness, rebellion and sin" (Exodus 34:6–7 NIV).

Did those men even know the name of the Man they had nailed to the cross—whose side they would pierce? Did they know His name was Jesus and that He was the Lamb of God, the One whom God had loved before the foundations of the world were even laid? It is likely none knew just how much they would need the forgiveness offered by the One hanging above them. They simply heard the words, "Father, forgive them, for they do not know what they are doing."

None understood that Jesus had taken on the role of advocate, defending the actions of those who had wronged Him. His teachings of "Love your enemies, bless those who curse you, do good to those who hate you, and pray for those who spitefully use you and per-secute you" (Matthew 5:44) were more than mere utterances; they were a lifestyle. It was an act of the will. He was teaching a world what true forgiveness really is.

Jesus taught that there was a relationship between forgiving and receiving God's forgiveness:

> "And whenever you stand praying, if you have anything against anyone, forgive him, that your Father in heaven may also forgive you your trespasses. But if you do not forgive, neither will your Father in heaven forgive your trespasses" (Mark 11:25–26).

The prayer for forgiveness on the cross was not meant to be the last act of a dying man; it was an example for His followers. As they had been forgiven, so were they to forgive those who sinned against them (see Matthew 6:9–13, the Lord's Prayer). Of course, it is often more readily talked about than practiced. It takes tremendous courage to exercise that kind of forgiveness. But it will bring you favor with God and the freedom to be healed emotionally and physically.

In Colossians 2:13–15, Paul wrote:

> And you, being dead in your trespasses and the uncircumcision of your flesh, He has made alive together with Him, having forgiven you all trespasses, having wiped out the handwriting of requirements that was against us, which was contrary to us. And He has taken it out of the way, having nailed it to the cross. Having disarmed principalities and

powers, He made a public spectacle of them, triumphing over them in it.

Evangelist and teacher Oswald Chambers wrote of forgiveness:

> Forgiveness is the divine miracle of grace. The cost to God was the Cross of Christ. To forgive sin, while remaining a holy God, this price had to be paid. Never accept a view of the fatherhood of God if it blots out the atonement. The revealed truth of God is that without the atonement He cannot forgive—He would contradict His nature if He did. The only way we can be forgiven is by being brought back to God through the atonement of the Cross. God's forgiveness is possible only in the supernatural realm.
>
> Compared with the miracle of the forgiveness of sin, the experience of sanctification is small. Sanctification is simply the wonderful expression or evidence of the forgiveness of sins in a human life. But the thing that awakens the deepest fountain of gratitude in a human being is that God has forgiven his sin. Paul never got away from this. Once you realize all that it cost God to forgive you, you will be held as in a vise, constrained by the love of God.[35]

Forgiveness is a matter of life and death for the forgiven. In John chapter 8, we read the story of the woman taken in adultery. It would fit into either the chapter on grace or the chapter on forgiveness in this book, but let's look at it here in terms of the grace of God's forgiveness.

It was a fall evening in Jerusalem at the conclusion of the Feast of Tabernacles. Jesus had spent the night on the Mount of Olives and had risen early to make His way to the Temple to connect with people gathering there in the dawn's light. Suddenly He heard a commotion—men shouting, the sound punctuated by the screams of a woman being manhandled up the rocky stairs and into the courtyard. She was exhausted from struggling to free herself from her captors. Tears stained her face, and her scanty clothing was dirty and bedraggled. Sheer terror distorted her features as she realized she was about to die at the hands of an angry mob.

The target of the scribes and Pharisees was sitting beneath the portico preparing to teach. Reaching Jesus, they hurled the woman down at His feet. As she cowered on the ground, the pain of her skinned hands and knees was nothing compared to the sentence that would be passed on her. Jesus made no overt move toward her or the men.

The charges brought by those hypocrites—and their purpose— are outlined in John 8:4–6:

> "Teacher, this woman was caught in adultery, in the very act. Now Moses, in the law, commanded us that such should be stoned. But what do You say?" This they said, testing Him, that they might have something of which to accuse Him.

Oh, how respectful were the self-righteous to the Man they were trying to trick; they called Him "Teacher." But how little they really knew about what He taught. The adultery charge could only be levied against the woman if she was married or betrothed, which was tantamount to marriage in those times. Since the Mosaic

Law required that a married adulterer be strangled, it is highly likely that this was a young woman engaged to be married. She was utterly humiliated as she lay on the ground before the crowd and her adversaries. I wonder if she knew the Man before whom they had dragged her. Did she know she was about to be judged by grace and forgiveness personified in the Lamb of God?

Were the men surprised that Jesus failed to react to their accusations? The Bible does not reveal how many times they asked Him the same question: "What do you say?" Surely at His silence her challengers began to grow frustrated with the calm and methodical Jesus. As their words whirled around Him, Jesus leaned over and began to write on the ground. We are not told what He wrote; only that He did.

Finally, the Righteous Judge began to speak words that must have chilled the hearts of those gathered:

> "He who is without sin among you, let him throw
> a stone at her first." And again He stooped down and
> wrote on the ground (vv. 7–8).

Now, the Law of Moses required that in order for a sentence to be carried out, there had to be two witnesses to bring the charges. Had the angry mob thought through the ramifications of the charges against the young woman? It would be their duty to pick up stones and take the life of the person on the ground before them. The men who had plotted against this woman in order to trap Jesus had likely not counted the entire cost of their actions. Were they coldhearted and brutal enough to carry out their own sentence against her? They were suddenly caught off guard. Now the proverbial ball was in their court.

Perhaps to give them time to think about the consequences of their actions, Jesus again leaned over and wrote on the ground:

> Then those who heard it, being convicted by their conscience, went out one by one, beginning with the oldest even to the last. And Jesus was left alone, and the woman standing in the midst (v. 9).

One by one the men began to slink away into the shadows. As the noise abated, the woman began to realize that something was happening. Raising her head slightly, she peeked around only to see that she was left alone with this Teacher, the one they called Jesus:

> When Jesus had raised Himself up and saw no one but the woman, He said to her, "Woman, where are those accusers of yours? Has no one condemned you?" She said, "No one, Lord." And Jesus said to her, "Neither do I condemn you; go and sin no more" (vv. 10–11).

Was it at that moment she understood—forgiveness was hers for the asking? She saw only kindness and peace in the eyes of the Man before her—not the disgust she had witnessed from her accusers earlier. She was still guilty of adultery, still worthy of death; now what would happen to her? Not one of her accusers was left to demand judgment. And in the whirl of controversy, she offered no justification for her sin, no declaration of her innocence, no defense of her actions. She stood totally exposed. And yet the One standing before her offered freedom from condemnation, but He required one thing from her—a repudiation of her sinful lifestyle.

The Mosaic Law could offer only condemnation and retalia-tion. She needed the same thing her accusers needed: forgiveness of sin and abundant grace. At no time did Jesus belittle this young woman for her immorality; not once did He shout angrily at her. He offered only hope and renewal; Jesus provided exactly what she was lacking—life and peace, grace and forgiveness.

Under the Law, the sacrifice of perfect, unblemished lambs was required to assuage God's anger and postpone His judgment. It was the person of Jesus Christ, the sinless Lamb of God who offered His life on the cross to become the once-for-all-time sacrifice for our sins. He died on the cross so that you and I may have forgiveness and eternal life and favor with our Father.

—DISCUSSION—
MATERIAL

1. Read Luke 6.

2. Have you been cheated by someone?

3. Can you really forgive and forget?

4. Why is the "forgetting" part so hard?

5. Why was Jesus' teaching on forgiveness so foreign to the Jews of His day?

6. What happens when we harbor unforgiveness in our heart?

7. What is the link between forgiveness and grace?

8. What do you think Jesus wrote on the ground?

9. How do you think the woman felt when she realized her accusers were gone?

—SCRIPTURES ON—
GOD'S FORGIVENESS

Let us then approach God's throne of grace with confidence, so that we may receive mercy and find grace to help us in our time of need.
HEBREWS 4:16 NIV

Come to me, all you who are weary and burdened, and I will give you rest.
MATTHEW 11:28 NIV

Cast your cares on the LORD
and he will sustain you;
he will never let the righteous be shaken.
PSALM 55:22 NIV

My dear children, I write this to you so that you will not sin. But if anybody does sin, we have an advocate with the Father—Jesus Christ, the Righteous One.
1 JOHN 2:1 NIV

If we confess our sins, he is faithful and just and will forgive us our sins and purify us from all unrighteousness.
1 JOHN 1:9 NIV

Repent, then, and turn to God, so that your sins may be wiped out, that times of refreshing may come from the Lord.
ACTS 3:19 NIV

Therefore, there is now no condemnation for those who are in Christ Jesus.
ROMANS 8:1 NIV

"Come now, let us settle the matter,"
says the LORD.
"Though your sins are like scarlet,
they shall be as white as snow;
though they are red as crimson,
they shall be like wool."
ISAIAH 1:18 NIV

Therefore, if anyone is in Christ, the new creation has
come: The old has gone, the new is here!
2 CORINTHIANS 5:17 NIV

In him we have redemption through his blood, the
forgiveness of sins, in accordance with the riches of God's
grace.
EPHESIANS 1:7 NIV

The Lord our God is merciful and forgiving, even though
we have rebelled against him.
DANIEL 9:9 NIV

CHAPTER TEN

GOD'S LOVE

For God so loved the world
that He gave His only begotten Son,
that whoever believes in Him
should not perish
but have everlasting life.

JOHN 3:16

FINDING A DEEP, SUSTAINING LOVE on earth is one of God's miracles. Mine came to me while attending Southwestern Bible College in Texas. I developed one very special friendship with a young woman, Carolyn. She had the sweetest smile I'd ever seen. Early in our relationship we became best friends and enjoyed that friendship for several years while she dated others. When Carolyn took me home to meet her parents I was captivated with my first real glimpse of a Christian home filled with love and grace. On Sunday mornings, her mom, Peggy, played Christian music while making lunch preparations. It was so peaceful in Peggy and Neil's home that I fell in love with Carolyn's parents immediately. I was also soon deeply in love with this special treasure whose name, Carolyn, means "joy." And that is just what she brought into my life—a glimpse of God's love and joy.

Sometimes it's not easy to demonstrate God's love to others. Several years ago, an Atlanta church honored an elderly former pastor by asking him to return to the pulpit and speak to the assembly. He delivered a profound message to the congregation. He said:

> When I was asked to come here today and talk to you, your pastor asked me to tell you what was the greatest lesson ever learned in my 50-odd years of preaching. I thought about it for a few days and boiled it down to just one thing that made the most difference in my life and sustained me through all my trials. The one thing that I could always rely on when tears and heartbreak and pain and fear and sorrow paralyzed me...the only thing that would comfort was this verse.
>
> "Jesus loves me this I know. For the Bible tells me so. Little ones to Him belong, we are weak but He is strong.... Yes, Jesus loves me.... The Bible tells me so."[36]

The truth of that children's song is expressed in every page of the Bible. It rings with the message of the love of God for His people. Moses witnessed it on Mount Sinai; Abraham encountered it in a ram caught in a bush; David sang of it on the hills of Judea; and God used the story of Hosea and his wayward wife, Gomer, to show His love for His wandering people.

The little Old Testament book of Hosea doesn't just tell us of God's love for Israel; the prophet lived it out in a way that would be difficult, if not impossible, for many. Hosea was instructed to find a wife, and not just any wife; he was to marry a prostitute, the basest of women. Hosea was to love with a God-like love a woman who perhaps would not reciprocate his affection. The prophet was to enter into a one-sided marital relationship. Jehovah wanted Hosea to love the wife he would choose with the same love that He had for Israel. This was to be about Hosea's unconditional love for her.

Ready to fulfill God's instruction, Hosea set out to find God's choice for him. He settled on a woman named Gomer—not a name we hear a lot today. Oddly, it means "complete." Much to Hosea's surprise and chagrin, he fell deeply in love with this woman. They married and had three children together. But one day the ordinariness of being a wife and mother got the better of Gomer and she abandoned her family only to return to the life of prostitution. Like many men—and women—today who have been betrayed by a spouse, Hosea took up the reins of parenthood and raised the children alone, all the while desperately lonely for the wife who had abandoned him.

God allowed this for a time, but one day He instructed Hosea to go out and search for Gomer, who by then had been abandoned by her lover and had sold herself into slavery. He searched all the back alleys and houses of ill-repute until he found his beloved wife— even though still an adulteress. How was it possible for Hosea to love Gomer that much—to love her desperately? We find the answer in Hosea 3:1, "Love your wife ... as the LORD loves" (NIV). In Ephesians 5:25, Paul wrote, "Husbands, love your wives, just as Christ also loved the church and gave Himself for her." The account of Hosea and Gomer is a remarkable illustration of God's great and gracious love, an outstanding biblical example of sacrificial love.

Hosea had finally found Gomer—dirty, unkempt, ill, and wretched, a mere shadow of her former self, yet he still loved her. He offered far more than she might have been worth on the auction block—fifteen shekels of silver and thirteen bushels of barley (see Hosea 3:2). I like to picture Hosea wrapping her in his cloak to protect her from prying eyes and then leading her home. Once there, he gave her specific instructions (verse 3):

> You shall stay with me many days; you shall not play the harlot, nor shall you have a man—so, too, will I be toward you.

Was it easy for Hosea to offer that kind of forgiveness to the one who had so betrayed him? Marriages are destroyed by far less than Hosea endured. But God had a lesson for Israel: He loved the people with an everlasting love. It was a mirror of God's constant love that reaches far beyond our sinfulness all the way to the Cross, where Love hung between heaven and earth.

In Hosea's day, the people of Israel kept returning to their sinful ways. In Hosea 6:4, God asks them, "O Ephraim, what shall I do to you? O Judah, what shall I do to you? For your faithfulness is like a morning cloud, And like the early dew it goes away." He reminded Israel of His constant love:

> When Israel was a child, I loved him; and out of Egypt I called My Son. I taught Ephraim to walk, taking them by their arms; but they did not know that I healed them. I drew them with gentle cords, with bands of love, and I was to them as those who take the yoke from their neck. I stooped and fed them (Hosea 11:1, 3–4).

Then God pleads with His people:

> O Israel, return to the LORD your God, for you
> have stumbled because of your iniquity (Hosea 14:1).

Oh, that we could express that kind of love and compassion, that kind of forgiveness! How can it be achieved? Only at the Cross of Christ; only by total surrender to God to allow Him to fill us to overflowing with His love and grace. It is the only way we can find help in times of trouble and bask in favor with God, as did Hosea.

In Ephesians 3:14–19, Paul wrote:

> For this reason I bow my knees to the Father of our Lord Jesus Christ, from whom the whole family in heaven and earth is named, that He would grant you, according to the riches of His glory, to be strengthened with might through His Spirit in the inner man, that Christ may dwell in your hearts through faith; that you, being rooted and grounded in love, may be able to comprehend with all the saints what *is* the width and length and depth and height—to know the love of Christ which passes knowledge; that you may be filled with all the fullness of God.

What joy! You and I are wholly loved by Jehovah. We are rooted and grounded, anchored—planted deeply in the bedrock of His love for us. We draw sustenance from our Father and His Word. It nurtures us; it is our divine food and living water that causes us to thrive. In Acts we read, "For in Him we live and move and have our being (17:28).

In West Texas during the winter months, tumbleweeds abound. They pile up against buildings, homes, or anywhere there is a barrier to impede their progress. Why? Because at certain times of the year, the plant detaches from the root system, dries up, and is completely at the mercy of the wind. So do we when we choose to separate ourselves from Christ. An old country preacher once said, "When we become separated from the Vine, we can wind up in a real pickle."

You and I find our resources from the all-encompassing love of God drawing our strength from Him. We are like the house built on a rock (see Matthew 7:25), able to withstand the storms of life because we know how great is our Father's love for us.

The word used in Ephesians 3:19 is the Greek word *agape*. It is defined as "selfless, sacrificial, unconditional love." Agape love always involves sacrifice; it is the kind of unconditional love that drove Jesus to the cross as a sacrifice for our sins. Agape love requires a decision on the part of the one who loves; it is a choice. God's kind of love means that I choose to love my unlovable mate, my wayward child, my unkind co-worker, my estranged parent. This kind of love is a charitable love, given not because it is deserved, but because God so loved us.

In his book *The Four Loves*, C. S. Lewis wrote:

> We are all receiving Charity. There is something in each of us that cannot be naturally loved. It is no one's fault if they do not so love it ... You might as well ask people to like the taste of rotten bread or the sound of a mechanical drill. We can be forgiven, and pitied, and loved in spite of it, with Charity; no other way. All who have good parents, wives, husbands,

or children, may be sure that at some times—and perhaps at all times in respect of some one particular trait or habit—they are receiving Charity, are loved not because they are lovable but because Love Himself [Christ] is in those who love them.[37]

God's agape love for His children is not something we can earn; it is fully undeserved, but freely given. In 1 John 3:1, we read, "Behold what manner of love the Father has bestowed on us, that we should be called children of God!" The writer continues in chapter 4, verse 10, "In this is love, not that we loved God, but that He loved us and sent His Son to be the propitiation [appeasement] for our sins."

Songwriter Ellis J. Crum wrote a song that speaks to this kind of agape love:

> He paid a debt He did not owe;
> I owed a debt I could not pay;
> I needed someone to wash my sins away.
> And, now, I sing a brand new song, "Amazing
> Grace."
> Christ Jesus paid a debt that I could never pay.[38]

The reason God sent His Son to earth can be summarized in six words in John 3:16: "For God so loved the world." Jesus came to earth because of love—the Father's love for His fallen creation. His love for all mankind directly affects you and me. We can now be restored to a loving relationship with Jehovah-Yasha—the Lord my Savior—because of Jesus' death on the cross. Now we are no longer enemies, but we are beloved friends.

The Bible reveals several crucial aspects of God's love in Ephesians 1:4–7:

- ✦ We were loved from "before the foundation of the world."

- ✦ We are to be "holy and without blame before Him in love."

- ✦ He "predestined us to adoption as sons."

- ✦ We have been made "accepted in the Beloved."

- ✦ We have "redemption through His blood."

- ✦ We have "forgiveness of sins."

Theologian Paul Berge said of such amazing love:

Our transformation, our conversion, makes us capable of feats of loving far beyond our mere human capacity—such as loving our enemies. How hard it is to love those who "revile you and persecute you and utter all kinds of evil against you falsely," as Jesus says (Matthew 5:11). And yet, the power of God's love makes it all possible. ... Through God's amazing grace, we ordinary Christians become capable of Olympic feats of love, lighting the world with love and bearing witness to God's extravagant love for us.[39]

Jesus said in John 13:35, "By this all will know that you are My disciples, if you have love for one another." When love is absent, all else is empty, without value.

In his booklet *The Mark of a Christian*, based on John 13:35, theologian Dr. Francis A. Schaeffer wrote:

> Our love will not be perfect, but it must be substantial enough for the world to be able to observe or it does not fit into the structure of the verses in John 13 and 17. And if the world does not observe this among true Christians, the world has a right to make the two awful judgments which these verses indicate: That we are not Christians, and that Christ was not sent by the Father.... Love...is the mark Christ gave Christians to wear before the world.[40]

Our very grasp of God's Word has no worth if love is not present. Our discipleship can be called into question by the very world we are trying to influence if love is missing from all we say and do. It all has no value without God's agape—sacrificial love at work in our lives.

In 1882 a blind Scottish preacher published a song that spoke of longing for the One from whose loving hands we could not be removed. His name was George Matheson; his message as timely today as it was then:

> O Love that wilt not let me go,
> I rest my weary soul in thee;
> I give thee back the life I owe,
> That in thine ocean depths its flow
> May richer, fuller be.[41]

The heart of man begs to be loved with this kind of love—to be loved despite our weaknesses and failures, to be completely accepted, highly esteemed, and to know that we have significance to someone. We want someone to be there to lift us up when we fail; to watch over us with kindness and compassion. That is the agape kind of love that God, the Father, has for His children. That is the kind of love that brings us favor with God.

—DISCUSSION—
MATERIAL

1. Read Hosea 3.

2. Hosea's obedience when told to marry a prostitute is amazing. How would you feel under the circumstances?

3. Would you obey God?

4. After the marriage and three children, Gomer left. Hosea was instructed to bring her home. Do you think it was easy for Hosea to offer that kind of forgiveness after having been so betrayed?

5. What was God trying to teach the children of Israel?

6. Name five crucial aspects of God's love.

7. How can the Church prove to the world that we are God's children?

—SCRIPTURES ON—
GOD'S LOVE

He that loveth not knoweth not God; for God is love.
1 JOHN 4:8 KJV

Nay, in all these things we are more than conquerors through him that loved us. For I am persuaded, that neither death, nor life, nor angels, nor principalities, nor powers, nor things present, nor things to come, nor height, nor depth, nor any other creature, shall be able to separate us from the love of God, which is in Christ Jesus our Lord.
ROMANS 8:37–39 KJV

Beloved, let us love one another: for love is of God; and every one that loveth is born of God, and knoweth God.
1 JOHN 4:7 KJV

In this was manifested the love of God toward us, because that God sent his only begotten Son into the world, that we might live through him. Herein is love, not that we loved God, but that he loved us, and sent his Son to be the propitiation for our sins. Beloved, if God so loved us, we ought also to love one another.
1 JOHN 4:9–11 KJV

There is no fear in love; but perfect love casteth out fear: because fear hath torment. He that feareth is not made perfect in love.
1 JOHN 4:18 KJV

And we have known and believed the love that God hath to us. God is love; and he that dwelleth in love dwelleth in God, and God in him.
1 JOHN 4:16 KJV

This is my commandment, that ye love one another, as I have loved you.

JOHN 15:12 KJV

But God commendeth his love toward us, in that, while we were yet sinners, Christ died for us.

ROMANS 5:8 KJV

A new commandment I give unto you, that ye love one another; as I have loved you, that ye also love one another.

JOHN 13:34–35 KJV

The LORD hath appeared of old unto me, saying, Yea, I have loved thee with an everlasting love: therefore with lovingkindness have I drawn thee.

JEREMIAH 31:3 KJV

But the fruit of the Spirit is love, joy, peace, longsuffering, gentleness, goodness, faith.

GALATIANS 5:22 KJV

✳

CHAPTER ELEVEN

GOD'S PEACE

And the peace of God, which surpasses all understanding,
will guard your hearts and minds through Christ Jesus.

PHILIPPIANS 4:7

PEACE! IT IS A MISSING COMMODITY in many lives today. Outside pressures and problems beset us—jobs, poor health, lack of funds, abusive situations, or family relationship issues. Headlines scream of terrorist attacks, rampant disease, and wars and rumors of wars around the world. Peace is in short supply, and yet in John 14:27, Jesus said:

> Peace I leave with you: My [own] peace I now give...to you. Not as the world gives do I give to you. Do not let your hearts be troubled, neither let them be afraid. [Stop allowing yourselves to be agitated and disturbed; and do not permit yourselves to be fearful and intimidated and cowardly and unsettled.] (AMP)

When we arise in the morning, we find ourselves fearful, irritated, and discouraged. Yet this is not the life God has for us. Second

Timothy 1:7 promises, "For God has not given us a spirit of fear, but of power and of love and of a sound mind."

Jesus has promised us a peace that passes all understanding, one utterly unlike anything the world offers. It is a peace that surrounds and sustains us even when our human reasoning screams, "Oh no! We're all going to die!" Fear will destroy us.

It was God's peace that I experienced following my encounter with Jesus at the age of eleven. As a child I was fearful because of my father's actions. I was shy and withdrawn. Anxiety, fear, worry, and hurt dogged my every step. I was ensnared by a spirit of rejection. I was unwanted and unloved—and I knew it. And then Jesus came to my rescue. When I embraced Him and dedicated my life to His service, I learned that the Jesus of whom I was taught in Sunday school was as real as the air I breathed, as close as the scarred skin on my back. As I recounted in chapter three, Jesus had called me "son," said He loved me and had a wonderful plan for my life. I knew firsthand how the woman in the Bible with the issue of blood must have felt when He called her "daughter" (see Mark 5). What indescribable peace and joy to know that I was the beloved son of God!

When faced with adversity, we can do one of two things—we can accept it as our lot in life, or we can overcome it through the peace of God and His Word. The moment in my life that I realized the Enemy was out to destroy me and my ministry, I did what God had told me to do: I got up and went—all the way to Israel. Doing God's will gave me the peace to overcome adversity. And then I began to worship God, to praise, to exalt my Creator. Praise dispelled the darkness and allowed the light of God's love to shine in and His peace to flood my being.

I have learned that peace is not the absence of conflict; it is having the courage to face the conflict and make the right choices. This is true in my life; it is true in yours. Peace and worry cannot occupy the same space. One forces the other to vacate. Our prayer should be:

> *Help me to wait patiently for the very best You have for me. Help me not to be ruled by fear but to lay hold of Your peace.*

It is all too easy to blame others for our problems—our parents, spouse, lack of schooling, physical ailments—to try to justify the way we are. But the apostle Paul said in Philippians 3:13, "Forgetting those things which are behind and reaching forward to those things which are ahead."

Although like many others, I was born into a home filled with abuse, alcohol, anger, and chaos, I had to learn to rely on the peace of God to see me through every difficult situation. Colossians 3:15 (AMP) says:

> And let the peace (soul harmony which comes) from Christ rule (act as umpire continually) in your hearts [deciding and settling with finality all questions that arise in your minds, in that peaceful state] to which as [members of Christ's] one body you were also called [to live]. And be thankful (appreciative), [giving praise to God always].

The vital component in having enduring peace is having God in one's life. Why? In John 16:33 (NASB), Jesus declares, "In Me you may have peace." Not in money; not in wealth; not in possessions;

not in fame—in God alone can true peace be found! Peace can be described as

> ...an inner sense of contentment and quietness, regardless of life's circumstances. It is steadfast confidence in our ever-faithful, immutable heavenly Father. It is the presence of joy in the midst of unhappiness. True peace does not merely dull our pain. A person who has genuine, godly peace can endure an avalanche of hardship and difficulty and still enjoy an inner peace that surpasses all human understanding. Why? Because it does not come from pleasant circumstances, nice events, or good things others may do for us. Instead, it is based on the fact that the Spirit of our holy, omnipotent, and never-changing God lives within us.[42]

How can we have peace in the midst of the storms of life? Peace is determined by our focus; if we focus on the problem, then peace flees. If the Believer focuses on the Problem-solver, he will be flooded with God's peace, which helps to calm the anxious heart.

Chicago businessman Horatio Spafford wrote one of the premier hymns about peace. On November 22, 1873, tragedy struck when a ship carrying Mrs. Spafford and their four daughters to England collided with the British ship *Lochearn*. Anna and the children's nanny struggled to get the children from their staterooms to the deck of the ship. The lifeboats were unusable, for they had been painted and had dried fast to the railing of the ship. As panic seized those onboard, Maggie stepped beside her mother and said, "Mama, God will take care of us." Annie added, "The sea is His and

He made it."[43] Only twelve minutes after the two ships rammed, the *Ville du Havre* sank to the bottom of the Atlantic, taking with it 226 people. Anna and fifty-six others survived. She was found bruised and unconscious atop a board floating in the Atlantic. Nicolet, the nanny, and the Spaffords' four daughters were among those swept to a watery grave, their bodies never recovered.

Anna told Bertha, a daughter born later to the couple, that "when she came back to consciousness in the boat, and she knew she had been recalled to life, her first realization was complete despair... Then, it was as if a voice spoke to her: 'You are spared for a purpose. You have work to do.'"[44]

Upon her arrival in Cardiff, Wales, where survivors were initially taken, Anna sent a cable that devastated Horatio Spafford. It said simply, "Saved alone." He immediately set sail for Wales to be reunited with his heartbroken wife. Once at sea, Spafford asked the captain to point out exactly where the *Ville du Havre* had sunk. When the ship crossed that fateful spot, he sat with pen in hand and wrote what was to become one of Christendom's most beloved hymns, "It Is Well With My Soul":

> When peace, like a river, attendeth my way,
> When sorrows like sea billows roll;
> Whatever my lot, Thou has taught me to say,
> It is well, it is well, with my soul.
>
> Though Satan should buffet, though trials
>   should come,
> Let this blest assurance control,
> That Christ has regarded my helpless estate,
> And hath shed His own blood for my soul.

My sin, oh, the bliss of this glorious thought!
My sin, not in part but the whole,
Is nailed to the cross, and I bear it no more,
Praise the Lord, praise the Lord, O my soul!

(Refrain)
It is well, with my soul,
It is well, it is well, with my soul.[45]

The Spaffords were finally reunited in Paris, where Anna had been taken to recuperate. God's peace ultimately overshadowed their trials, tribulations, and losses. They would eventually sell their possessions and move to Jerusalem in order to help the growing Jewish community in the city.

In Philippians 4:6–7, the apostle Paul tells us:

> Be anxious for nothing, but in everything by prayer and supplication, with thanksgiving, let your requests be made known to God; and the peace of God, which surpasses all understanding, will guard your hearts and minds through Christ Jesus.

It sounds as though Paul is being negative, but that is far from the truth. He is encouraging Believers to root out any hint of anxiety that may produce worry. Such fretfulness causes our hearts to be filled with the fear that God is not able to handle whatever the problem might be and wreaks havoc with our trust in the One who can bring total peace into any situation.

In these verses, the apostle defines the illness—anxiety, fear, apprehension. But he doesn't just leave us with the diagnosis. He says God has made available to you and me a divine gift: the secret to peace as a sure prescription to cure what ails us: prayer, supplication, and thanksgiving. Paul had come to this conclusion, not as a free man, but as a prisoner awaiting sentence. He had every reason to be nervous, every right to be concerned; and yet he says, "Don't worry!" The positive result of casting our burdens on Him is absolute peace and blessed favor with God.

Daniel 6 is the story of God's peace that passes understanding at work in the life of the writer. At that juncture in his life, Daniel was no longer a young man; it is likely that he was nearing ninety years of age. We can see from his longevity in the Babylonian and then the Medo-Persian empires Daniel was a man of wisdom, a dynamic leader, and a capable administrator. He was God's man for that time and in that place. God had turned the heart of Darius, the new ruler in Babylon, toward a Hebrew man who was then elevated to a strategic place of authority.

It was not long before the Enemy raised his ugly head, and Daniel was the target of Satan's venom. Soon others in the court were plotting:

> So the governors and satraps sought to find some charge against Daniel concerning the kingdom; but they could find no charge or fault, because he was faithful; nor was there any error or fault found in him. Then these men said, "We shall not find any charge against this Daniel unless we find it against him concerning the law of his God" (Daniel 6:4–5).

The accusers could find no fault in Daniel; his life was exemplary. He was a member in good standing of the Fellowship of the

Offenders—his dedication to Yahweh had caused offense to the Babylonians. They had to resort to subterfuge in order to trap their rival. Daniel was known abroad for his custom of praying with his face toward Jerusalem three times each day. So his adversaries took advantage of Daniel's routine and approached the king:

> King Darius, live forever! All the governors of the kingdom, the administrators and satraps, the counselors and advisors, have consulted together to establish a royal statute and to make a firm decree, that whoever petitions any god or man for thirty days, except you, O king, shall be cast into the den of lions. Now, O king, establish the decree and sign the writing, so that it cannot be changed, according to the law of the Medes and Persians, which does not alter (Daniel 6:6–8).

Sneaky, weren't they? And, of course, the king was flattered by all this attention. Who wouldn't want to be God for a month! Obviously, Darius succumbed to the temptation and signed the decree. He was swept away on a tide of ego and pressed his signet ring into wax on the document that would become law, one which could not be changed. The thing was done—bow to any God except Darius and become Meow Mix® for the captive lions.

When Daniel heard of the new law, did he begin to look for a secret place to pray? No! Verse 10 says:

> Now when Daniel knew that the writing was signed, he went home. And in his upper room, with

his windows open toward Jerusalem, he knelt down on his knees three times that day, and prayed and gave thanks before his God, as was his custom since early days (Daniel 6:10).

Peace reigned in Daniel's life; he was no "secret servant." God had been faithful to him, and he had no reason to doubt. Either he would be preserved in the lions' den, or not, but Daniel was committed to doing the will of God. Daniel knelt in his window in open view of passersby, his face toward the Holy City, according to 1 Kings 8:47–49 (NLT):

> But in that land of exile, they might turn to you in repentance and pray, "We have sinned, done evil, and acted wickedly." If they turn to you with their whole heart and soul in the land of their enemies and pray toward the land you gave to their ancestors— toward this city you have chosen, and toward this Temple I have built to honor your name—then hear their prayers and their petition from heaven where you live, and uphold their cause.

Seeing Daniel in earnest prayer, the instigators smugly and triumphantly scurried to the king:

> Have you not signed a decree that every man who petitions any god or man within thirty days, except you, O king, shall be cast into the den of lions? ... That Daniel, who is one of the captives from Judah, does

not show due regard for you, O king, or for the decree that you have signed, but makes his petition three times a day (Daniel 6:12, 13).

The combination of envy and enmity produced exultation from those who had devised the plan. The trap had been set, and Daniel had fallen into it; enemy vanquished—or so they thought.

The king likely felt as though he had been hit with a left hook to the jaw! He was stunned by this turn of events: A man he greatly admired was now in dire straits because of Darius' egotism.

Daniel was quickly arrested and led to the lair where the lions were confined. He was flung inside, and the mouth of the den was sealed. Let me assure you that these were not cute little lion cubs, nor were there only one or two in the den. There were a sufficient number of lions to rip Daniel to shreds and devour him in a matter of minutes.

Darius then sealed the covering with his signet ring and returned to the palace. So distressed was the king that he spent the night wordlessly fasting. In his sleeplessness he failed to summon the musicians, or the dancing girls, or indulge in other diversions. The Bible says, "And he could not sleep." I believe he spent the night pacing in his bedchamber. At the earliest opportunity, he burst forth from his room and went in search of an answer:

> At the first light of dawn, the king got up and hurried to the lions' den. When he came near the den, he called to Daniel in an anguished voice, "Daniel, servant of the living God, has your God, whom you serve continually, been able to rescue you from the

lions?" Daniel answered, "May the king live forever! My God sent his angel, and he shut the mouths of the lions. They have not hurt me, because I was found innocent in his sight. Nor have I ever done any wrong before you, Your Majesty" (Daniel 6:19–22 NIV).

It seems that every seed Daniel had sown into the king's life erupted at the mouth of the lions' den in the words, "Daniel, servant of the living God, has your God, whom you serve..." He wanted to know if everything Daniel had said to him was true. Could the living God deliver, do the miraculous, save the endangered? Darius had his answer as soon as he heard the words, "My God sent His angel, and he shut the mouths of the lions."

There is no record that Daniel offered any argument to the king before he was led away to the lions' den; only after God had vindicated him and saved him from the jaws of the ferocious beasts did he offer any defense. He knew he had been innocent of anything other than obedience to Jehovah-Shalom, the God who was Daniel's peace in the midst of the ravening lions. Daniel had sought the kingdom of God and had been rewarded. Daniel's persistence in prayer won the favor of the king, but more importantly, it brought an outward sign of Daniel's favor with God.

—DISCUSSION—
MATERIAL

1. Read John 14.

2. How can a Believer have peace in the midst of today's global turmoil?

3. Define peace.

4. What is the vital component to having peace in your life?

5. What is the secret to peace according to Philippians 4:6?

6. Have you ever been asked to deny your belief in Christ?

7. How do we often respond when falsely accused?

8. How can we have peace that passes understanding?

— SCRIPTURES ON —
GOD'S PEACE

Blessed are the peacemakers: for they shall be called the children of God.
MATTHEW 5:9 KJV

And the peace of God, which passeth all understanding, shall keep your hearts and minds through Christ Jesus.
PHILIPPIANS 4:7 KJV

Now the Lord of peace himself give you peace always by all means. The Lord be with you all.
2 THESSALONIANS 3:16 KJV

Peace I leave with you, my peace I give unto you: not as the world giveth, give I unto you. Let not your heart be troubled, neither let it be afraid.
JOHN 14:27 KJV

Thou wilt keep him in perfect peace, whose mind is stayed on thee: because he trusteth in thee.
ISAIAH 26:3 KJV

These things I have spoken unto you, that in me ye might have peace. In the world ye shall have tribulation: but be of good cheer; I have overcome the world.
JOHN 16:33 KJV

Those things, which ye have both learned, and received, and heard, and seen in me, do: and the God of peace shall be with you.
PHILIPPIANS 4:9 KJV

Now the God of hope fill you with all joy and peace in believing, that ye may abound in hope, through the power of the Holy Ghost.
ROMANS 15:13 KJV

For the mountains shall depart, and the hills be removed; but my kindness shall not depart from thee, neither shall the covenant of my peace be removed, saith the LORD that hath mercy on thee.

ISAIAH 54:10 KJV

Grace to you, and peace, from God our Father and the Lord Jesus Christ.

PHILEMON 1:3 KJV

And let the peace of God rule in your hearts, to the which also ye are called in one body; and be ye thankful.

COLOSSIANS 3:15 KJV

Now the God of peace be with you all. Amen.

ROMANS 15:33 KJV

And all thy children shall be taught of the LORD; and great shall be the peace of thy children.

ISAIAH 54:13 KJV

Depart from evil, and do good; seek peace, and pursue it.

PSALM 34:14 KJV

To Titus, mine own son after the common faith: Grace, mercy, and peace, from God the Father and the Lord Jesus Christ our Saviour.

TITUS 1:4 KJV

For ye shall go out with joy, and be led forth with peace: the mountains and the hills shall break forth before you into singing, and all the trees of the field shall clap their hands.

ISAIAH 55:12 KJV

But he was wounded for our transgressions, he was bruised for our iniquities: the chastisement of our peace was upon him; and with his stripes we are healed.

ISAIAH 53:5 KJV

CHAPTER TWELVE

GOD'S ANOINTING
FOR THE IMPOSSIBLE

"For with God nothing will be impossible."

LUKE 1:37

SHIRA JOY, OUR SECOND CHILD, whose name in Hebrew means "Song of Joy," was born prematurely and weighed only three and a half pounds at birth. The doctor who delivered her told us she might not survive. After Carolyn was settled in her hospital room, I stumbled down the hall to the tiny chapel and fell on my face before God to intercede for our baby girl. As I prayed to Jehovah-Rophe—the Lord who Heals—a verse from Psalm 118 flooded my spirit. The psalmist, in verse 17, boldly declares: "I shall not die, but live, and declare the works of the LORD."

Our precious baby girl survived but was left with some physical frailties. When she started school, Shira had difficulty keeping up with the other students. Noticing her frustration, I devised a plan to help her. Each night before she dropped off to sleep, I sat by her bedside and quoted scripture to her, reminding her that she was strong in the Lord. For example, I would quote Ephesians 6:10:

"Finally, my brethren, be strong in the Lord and in the power of His might." She began to memorize those verses and quote them to herself. Soon, she was attempting physical challenges she had been afraid to even try. Before long, the entire family began to notice a remarkable difference in Shira's attitude as well as in her physical strength and endurance. The result? Shira grew into a strong, intelligent, capable young woman.

What the doctor had thought impossible, God said, "For I am the Lord who heals you!"

My dear friend and mentor, the late David Wilkerson, wrote:

> God has decreed that all his promises are conveyed through the prayer of faith. God knows all — he knows what we need before we ask — and he has promised to do the impossible. Yet it all comes to pass through prayer. Christ was the fullness of God, the very fulfillment of all God's promises. Still, he spent nights in prayer, showing his dependence on the Father. ... Do you see it? God said, "I will do it. I will answer you, deliver you. But first you will ask me, seek me." The promise was given, but the people had to lay hold of it by prayer and seeking God.[46]

I grew up watching the old television series *Mission Impossible*. The earlier shows were a little less high-tech than the current movie versions, but the premise was the same. The show's opening sequence was identified by the head of the team receiving instructions via a recorded message. It always ended with, "Your mission, should you decide to accept it..." and then concluded with the mysterious tape self-destructing.[47]

There are times when each of us feels as if our life is an impossible undertaking. When sickness, broken relationships, joblessness, divorce, or death come our way, we encounter unbearable issues. At these times, we are often faced with questions and no answers; seemingly impossible situations. Author Elisabeth Elliott wrote: "Faith does not eliminate questions. But faith knows where to take them."[48]

Talk about impossible situations! The prophet Elijah, forced to run for his life from King Ahab and Queen Jezebel, made the long trek from his cave in the mountains to the coastal town of Zarephath. There he was given the assignment to stay with a widow who had one son. It was there that God's miraculous provision of flour and oil made the difference between life and death. The the inconceivable happened:

> ...the son of the woman who owned the house became sick. And his sickness was so serious that there was no breath left in him (1 Kings 17:17).

In agony, she confronts the prophet:

> "What have I to do with you, O man of God? Have you come to me to bring my sin to remembrance, and to kill my son?"

Remember, there was still flour in the bin and oil in the carafe; there was still bread on the table because of Jehovah's provision. God had supplied her need for food to sustain her family, but still the unthinkable happened and she responded with bitter tears. Elijah countered with action. He took the child from her arms and climbed the stairs to his room on the roof of the house. There the prophet laid the boy on his cot and raised his face to heaven:

> And he stretched himself out on the child three times, and cried out to the LORD and said, "O LORD my God, I pray, let this child's soul come back to him." Then the LORD heard the voice of Elijah; and the soul of the child came back to him, and he revived. And Elijah took the child and brought him down from the upper room into the house, and gave him to his mother. And Elijah said, "See, your son lives!" Then the woman said to Elijah, "Now by this I know that you are a man of God, and that the word of the LORD in your mouth is the truth" (vv. 21–24).

All too often people blame God when bad things happen. Blessings will bring the response of "See what I've done," or "I reached my goal." Bad things, on the other hand, are frequently referred to as an "act of God." Writer Michelle Wallace penned these timeless words:

> I am convinced that darkness is the perfect backdrop for the light. The things that are impossible for man are possible with God.[49]

Faced with an excruciating situation, Elijah turned to the God of the possible, and the result was restoration. The prophet refused to focus on the dead child; he turned instead to the giver of life, the One who with His very breath created man. I am reminded of the poem "Footprints in the Sand." The anonymous writer bemoaned the fact that at the most difficult times of life when he or she thought God was walking alongside, only one set of footprints could be seen in the sands of time. The poem ends with:

> The Lord replied, "My precious, precious child. I love you, and I would never, never leave you during your times of trial and suffering. When you saw only one set of footprints, it was then that I carried you."[50]

When an impossible situation arises, God is there:

> To comfort all who mourn, to console those who mourn in Zion, to give them beauty for ashes, the oil of joy for mourning, the garment of praise for the spirit of heaviness (Isaiah 61:2b–3).

A very similar event occurred in the life of Jesus. In Luke 7:11–17 He and His disciples were traveling across Judea when they arrived at the village of Nain. As they entered the town, a crowd of mourners was leaving the city to bury the only son of a widow. The mother was inconsolable, and those surrounding her wailed because of her sad predicament:

> When the Lord saw her, He had compassion on her and said to her, "Do not weep" (v. 13).

As at other times in His ministry, the crowd must have rolled their eyes in disbelief. Who was this stranger that dared tell a grieving mother not to weep! But then the very air became charged with hope as He approached the funeral platform and called, "Young man, I say to you, arise" (v. 14).

The mourners, those who remained after the young man sat up and took a deep breath, were most certainly speechless! Or perhaps someone in the crowd began to sing verses from Psalm 30:

> You have turned for me my mourning into danc-
> ing; You have put off my sackcloth and clothed me
> with gladness, to the end that my glory may sing
> praise to You and not be silent. O LORD my God, I
> will give thanks to You forever (vv. 11–12).

If ever there was an impossible man, it was the apostle Paul! His early mission in life as Saul was to rid the world of those hated Christians. Acts chapter 9 relates the story of a man bent on murder and mayhem:

> Then Saul, still breathing threats and murder
> against the disciples of the Lord, went to the high
> priest and asked letters from him to the synagogues
> of Damascus, so that if he found any who were of the
> Way, whether men or women, he might bring them
> bound to Jerusalem (vv. 1–2).

Saul was a scoundrel of the first order—proud, self-righteous, conceited, and overbearing. He described himself in Philippians 3 as "circumcised the eighth day, of the stock of Israel, of the tribe of Benjamin, a Hebrew of the Hebrews; concerning the law, a Pharisee; concerning zeal, persecuting the church; concerning the righteousness which is in the law, blameless" (vv. 5–6). His pedigree was impeccable, or so he thought, until he met Jesus on the road to Damascus. Then he admitted in that same chapter:

> But what things were gain to me, these I have counted loss for Christ. Yet indeed I also count all things loss for the excellence of the knowledge of Christ Jesus my Lord, for whom I have suffered the loss of all things, and count them as rubbish, that I may gain Christ and be found in Him, not having my own righteousness, which is from the law, but that which is through faith in Christ, the righteousness which is from God by faith; that I may know Him and the power of His resurrection, and the fellowship of His sufferings, being conformed to His death, if, by any means, I may attain to the resurrection from the dead (vv. 7–11).

Paul found favor with God and became an apostle of note and the writer of many of the New Testament epistles. What a transformation—from murderer to missionary, from blasphemer to blessed! He had been given full authority by the High Priest to track down Believers, drag them from their homes, and have them executed. He was zealous for the law—then he encountered Grace personified in Christ Jesus, who called him out, "Saul, Saul, why are you persecuting Me?" (Acts 9:4)

That was the end for Saul and the beginning of a new life for Paul, the Believer, the follower of Christ, the radical apostle. His life was changed; his outlook was changed; his message was changed. There were likely some Christians in Paul's day that saw him as a hopeless case, a mission impossible. But God is the God of new beginnings.

Things certainly didn't always go smoothly for Paul after he committed his life to Christ. He wrote in his second letter to the Corinthians, chapter 11, verses 24–28:

> From the Jews five times I received forty stripes minus one. Three times I was beaten with rods; once I was stoned; three times I was shipwrecked; a night and a day I have been in the deep; in journeys often, in perils of waters, in perils of robbers, in perils of my own countrymen, in perils of the Gentiles, in perils in the city, in perils in the wilderness, in perils in the sea, in perils among false brethren; in weariness and toil, in sleeplessness often, in hunger and thirst, in fastings often, in cold and nakedness—besides the other things, what comes upon me daily: my deep concern for all the churches.

Yet despite that, he could also say:

> ... nevertheless I am not ashamed, for I know whom I have believed and am persuaded that He is able to keep what I have committed to Him until that Day (2 Timothy 1:12b).

Paul enjoyed full favor with God. He knew that "all things work together for good to those who love God, to those who are the called according to His purpose" (Romans 8:28). He discovered that God had a plan for his life, one that he had never considered.

Paul thought that by his works he could save himself, and then he discovered:

> For by grace you have been saved through faith,
> and that not of yourselves; it is the gift of God, not
> of works, lest anyone should boast (Ephesians 2:8–9).

Paul truly met the God of the impossible—the One who was born as a baby, lived as a man, suffered death on the cross, rose again the third day, and now sits at the right hand of God, making intercession for His beloved children.

The impossible often begins with one small step. When God wanted to create Adam, He began with a handful of dust. Moses was sent to challenge Pharaoh with a walking stick; Samson killed thousands of Philistines with the jawbone of a donkey (see Judges 15); Jesus fed the multitudes with a couple of fish and five loaves of bread. Small beginnings to be sure! When He sent David to conquer a giant, the shepherd didn't take a cannon; he took five small stones. When God sent His Son to earth, He wasn't sent to a metropolis, but to the small, backwater hamlet of Bethlehem. In Zechariah 4:10 (NLT), the prophet says, "Do not despise these small beginnings, for the LORD rejoices to see the work begin." Do you think your ideas are too small to succeed? Give them to God and let Him anoint you for the impossible.

This is the entire story of Abraham's life. God took an impossible situation and created an entire nation of people. Abraham was seventy-five years old when God called him to pack up and head to a land that would become home for him and his descendants. God promised him that his progeny would be like the stars in the sky and the sands on the seashore. What could He have been thinking?

Abraham and his wife had no children and no hope of having any because of their ages. Until one day, the God of the impossible anointed a now ninety-year-old man to father a child. The day finally came that Sarah awoke to find that she was pregnant in her old age. She who had laughed at the pronouncement that she would bear a child—she who had intervened and proposed her own plan for an heir (see Genesis 16)—Sarah was now carrying Isaac, the son of promise. Not only had God taken away her barrenness, He provided strength to carry the child to term and to bring him forth.

God still does the impossible: He redeems us and calls us to new life in Him. That, my friend, is the greatest example of favor *with* God.

—DISCUSSION—
MATERIAL

1. Read 1 Kings 17.

2. What role does prayer play in achieving the impossible?

3. How did the widow respond to the death of her son?

4. Why do we tend to blame God when bad things happen?

5. Paul was quite a character before he found salvation in Jesus Christ. Do you know anyone who was dramatically changed by an encounter with Jesus?

6. How was your own life changed when you met the Lord?

7. Have you ever been prompted to step out in faith? What was the outcome?

8. Does God still do the impossible today?

—SCRIPTURES ON—
GOD'S ANOINTING FOR THE IMPOSSIBLE

But the anointing which ye have received of him abideth in you, and ye need not that any man teach you: but as the same anointing teacheth you of all things, and is truth, and is no lie, and even as it hath taught you, ye shall abide in him.

1 JOHN 2:27 KJV

The Spirit of the Lord is upon me, because he hath anointed me to preach the gospel to the poor; he hath sent me to heal the brokenhearted, to preach deliverance to the captives, and recovering of sight to the blind, to set at liberty them that are bruised.

LUKE 4:18 KJV

Is any sick among you? let him call for the elders of the church; and let them pray over him, anointing him with oil in the name of the Lord.

JAMES 5:14 KJV

The Spirit of the Lord GOD is upon me; because the LORD hath anointed me to preach good tidings unto the meek; he hath sent me to bind up the brokenhearted, to proclaim liberty to the captives, and the opening of the prison to them that are bound

ISAIAH 61:1–11 KJV

And they cast out many devils, and anointed with oil many that were sick, and healed them.

MARK 6:13 KJV

Then Samuel took the horn of oil, and anointed him in the midst of his brethren: and the Spirit of the LORD came upon David from that day forward. So Samuel rose up, and went to Ramah.

1 SAMUEL 16:13 KJV

And it shall come to pass in that day, that his burden shall be taken away from off thy shoulder, and his yoke from off thy neck, and the yoke shall be destroyed because of the anointing.
ISAIAH 10:27 KJV

Then shalt thou take the anointing oil, and pour it upon his head, and anoint him.
EXODUS 29:7 KJV

But Jesus beheld them, and said unto them, With men this is impossible; but with God all things are possible.
MATTHEW 19:26 KJV

For with God nothing shall be impossible.
LUKE 1:37 KJV

But without faith it is impossible to please him: for he that cometh to God must believe that he is, and that he is a rewarder of them that diligently seek him.
HEBREWS 11:6 KJV

CHAPTER THIRTEEN

PURSUING GOD

But seek first the kingdom of God and His righteousness,
and all these things shall be added to you.

MATTHEW 6:33

FOR THE TWELVE YEARS OF MY MINISTRY, I had felt inferior; no matter how hard I worked I felt I should have been working harder. No matter how little I slept I felt I should be awake and doing more. Depression descended like a heavy blanket. I drew more deeply inside myself as I refused to trust anyone, afraid to share my fears.

A black cloud of depression settled over me, and my ministry fell apart. I stopped preaching and would sit for hours on the steps of our headquarters building—trying to pray, but most often succumbing to the tears that constantly threatened. I was defeated and despondent and had descended into a living hell.

In the midst of my physical turmoil I went to an ophthalmologist for an eye examination. During the visit he insisted that I hold my head straight. I didn't want to confess that for several months I had not been able to do that successfully. The more he urged me to straighten up, the more my head began to shake uncontrollably. I was mortified and had no idea what was happening to me.

The visit to the eye doctor began what seemed like a never-ending trek from ophthalmologist to neurologist and back to the ophthalmologist—all with no success. Each in turn found nothing wrong with my neck and told me the same thing: My neck problem probably stemmed from some kind of emotional issue. I began to accept what seemed to be the obvious diagnosis because of the stress I had undergone.

When I spoke before an audience, I would have to physically hold my head with my hand to keep it from shaking. It got so bad that embarrassment and humiliation assailed me just at the mention of preaching. At one point, because my head shook so badly, I was accused of being drunk even though I never touched alcohol. Finally I could handle it no longer; I cancelled all pending meetings. I was diagnosed as having a type of spasmodic torticollis dystonia—a disease that also plagued my mother.

I called my staff together and encouraged them to find other jobs. I literally watched as the ministry God had given me became smoke and then crumbled into ashes before my eyes. In my disappointment, discouragement, and defeat, and without consulting God, I put our headquarters building up for sale and decided there was nothing left for me but to leave the ministry and take my family home to Texas. I could no longer handle the pain, rejection, humiliation, and shame.

My depression and despondency drove me to secretly take a real estate course in preparation for an entirely new career, and yet ultimately I couldn't escape the call of God on my life. Though I was no longer pursuing God's calling, He never stopped pursuing me. His love, literally, would not let me go.

As Believers we are all seeking something, but are the things we seek worthwhile? The road through life can be rocky, but there is One who has promised to be with us. Jesus said in Matthew 28:20, "And lo, I am with you always, even to the end of the age." Amen.

David, the shepherd king, pursued God from an early age—from his days of watching over his father's sheep and crafting songs about God's love and provision. In doing so, he found enormous favor with God. How do we know he sought God? He tells us in Psalm 63:1–2, 8:

> O God, You are my God; early will I seek You; my soul thirsts for You; my flesh longs for You in a dry and thirsty land where there is no water. So I have looked for You in the sanctuary, to see Your power and Your glory. ... My soul follows close behind You; Your right hand upholds me.

Pastor Tommy Tenney's book *The God Chasers: My Soul Follows Hard After Thee*, offers this description of what it means to pursue God:

> A God Chaser is a person whose passion for God's presence presses him to chase the impossible in hopes that the uncatchable might catch him.[51]

Tenney goes on to mention David and Paul, along with other more contemporary God Chasers, and adds:

> These are people whose relentless, passionate pursuit of Christ often made them appear foolish in the eyes of others. Yet, having tasted His goodness and

glimpsed the invisible, they could be satisfied with nothing less.[52]

In Acts 13:22 God said of him, "I have found David the son of Jesse, a man after My own heart, who will do all My will." David had a heart that followed after God; he chose that path, and even though he oft-times struggled with sin, David never ceased to pursue Jehovah.

The future king of Judah was an obedient child who performed the tasks set before him, whether tending sheep or catering lunch to his brothers. His job in the hills was isolated, tedious, and difficult, but David's body of work in the Psalms is indicative of a mind that remained focused on Jehovah, from whom came his help. He had gained an intimate knowledge of the Creator and totally trusted His faithfulness. When called upon by his earthly father, David responded quickly and without question. When his flock was challenged by predators, he called upon the Source of his strength for help. David's attitude would stand him in good stead when challenged by the giant, Goliath, or by his predecessor to the throne, King Saul.

David enjoyed great acclaim for a time after defeating the giant from Gath, but jealousy entered the heart of the king and he began a campaign designed to destroy the young man who had saved Israel. David was stalked like a criminal, hid in caves, took refuge in enemy territory, rejected opportunities to kill his adversary, and loved Jonathan, Saul's son, more than a brother.

The man who had been anointed as the future king had become a hunted outlaw with a price on his head. Day and night for years Saul dogged David, just waiting for the moment when David would become vulnerable. The desire of Saul's heart was to plunge his spear through the man he deemed his adversary. And even more doggedly than Saul pursued him, David pursued God, unwilling to lose sight of the One who was his "strength and shield" (see Psalm 28:7).

After years of evading the jealousy-crazed Saul, a betrayed and embattled, lonely and weary David took refuge in the cave of Adullum:

> And every one that was in distress, and every one that was in debt, and every one that was discontented, gathered themselves unto him; and he became a captain over them: and there were with him about four hundred men (1 Samuel 22:2 KJV).

There was no self-promotion for David. He was isolated in a wintry cavern. Things were going from bad to worse, but David refused to become a victim of "cave mentality." He was surrounded by the distressed (those under pressure or stress), by debtors (people who could not pay their bills), and by the discontent (those bitter of soul). Did he fall into self-pity? Not David! He turned the pursuit into an opportunity to gather those men around him and teach them how to pursue Jehovah in order to become mighty men of valor!

Have you ever found yourself in a pit of despair—distressed, in debt, and discontented—hoping against hope that someone would come around and point you in the right direction? Step out of the darkness and into the brilliant light of God's Word! Abandon the pity party for a praise party. Begin to pursue a deeper relationship with God instead of surrendering to the pressure of pursuit. Give yourself over to the mission of finding favor with God.

David found himself in a cave, but the cave was not in him! David was content to wait for Jehovah to elevate him to a place of honor. So the anointed shepherd king and giant killer assumed the mantle of teacher and began to train his troops for spiritual and physical war.

David's passion in life was to have favor with God, to prepare a dwelling place for Jehovah in his heart and in Jerusalem. This seed was planted when he was a young shepherd boy; it was watered by Samuel's anointing; and matured by Saul's pursuit. David developed a heart attitude that moved God to action and produced favor with the King of Kings. He pursued God even when homeless and in great distress. He knew that no matter the question, the answer was Jehovah-'Ez-Lami—the Lord my Strength.

Like David, our focus should be on the quest for a deeper and more meaningful relationship with our heavenly Father. We should seek His presence, for it is there that, as David said of God in Psalm 16:11:

> You will show me the path of life; in Your presence is fullness of joy; at Your right hand are pleasures forevermore.

How do we develop a desire to pursue God? It is through communication with Him. As you and I spend time in His presence, we position ourselves to receive His favor and His grace. David, in Psalm 27:4, wrote of what was most important to him as a seeker, as a pursuer of Jehovah:

> One thing I have desired of the LORD, that will I seek: that I may dwell in the house of the LORD all

the days of my life, to behold the beauty of the LORD, and to inquire in His temple.

David longed for the presence of God to surround him and he craved the blessing of Jehovah on his life; he coveted the relationship he knew would come with spending time in His presence and valued above all the closeness he found with the Lord, his Shepherd. It is so easy in this life to get sidetracked in the pursuit of things—wealth, fame, the perfect job, house, or mate—that we fail to stop and spend time in the presence of God. Solomon, said to be the wisest of all men, was perhaps also the greatest seeker of pleasure. He said in Ecclesiastes 2:3–10:

> I searched in my heart how to gratify my flesh with wine, while guiding my heart with wisdom, and how to lay hold on folly, till I might see what was good for the sons of men to do under heaven all the days of their lives. I made my works great, I built myself houses, and planted myself vineyards. I made myself gardens and orchards, and I planted all kinds of fruit trees in them. I made myself water pools from which to water the growing trees of the grove. I acquired male and female servants, and had servants born in my house. Yes, I had greater possessions of herds and flocks than all who were in Jerusalem before me. I also gathered for myself silver and gold and the special treasures of kings and of the provinces. I acquired male and female singers, the delights of the sons of men, and musical instruments of all kinds. So I became great and excelled more than all who were

before me in Jerusalem. Also my wisdom remained
with me. Whatever my eyes desired I did not keep
from them. I did not withhold my heart from any
pleasure, for my heart rejoiced in all my labor; and
this was my reward from all my labor.

What a waste—a life given to the pursuit of pleasure rather than
the pursuit of God! David had learned the value of beholding the
beauty of the Lord, of seeking Him. He knew that God wanted a man
whose heart was submitted to Him. When David lost sight of that
pursuit and sinned with Bathsheba, he suffered the consequences
of his actions—the death of their first son. Likewise, because Adam
and Eve had sinned in the garden of Eden, God elected to pay the
ultimate price—the death of His Son.

But with his life dedicated to pursuing God, David finally
understood exactly what God wanted:

> For You do not desire sacrifice, or else I would give
> it; You do not delight in burnt offering. The sacrifices
> of God are a broken spirit, a broken and a contrite
> heart—these, O God, You will not despise (Psalm
> 51:16–17).

You and I can rest assured that God rewards those who diligently seek Him.

David wrote in Psalm 91:14–16:

> Because he has set his love upon Me, therefore I
> will deliver him; I will set him on high, because he
> has known My name. He shall call upon Me, and I

will answer him; I will be with him in trouble; I will deliver him and honor him. With long life I will satisfy him, and show him My salvation.

Psalm 34 gives us the perfect outline for pursuing God. There are several steps that the psalmist suggests we follow. In verses 1–3 he tells us that we are to applaud the majesty of Jehovah-Bara—God our Creator:

> I will bless the LORD at all times; His praise shall continually be in my mouth. My soul shall make its boast in the LORD; the humble shall hear of it and be glad. Oh, magnify the LORD with me, and let us exalt His name together.

David's worship was a conscious choice of his will. He was determined to worship, to bless the Lord—not just when he felt like it or circumstances dictated. Just as love is an act of the will, so is praise. David made a deliberate decision with no thought of what others might or might not do. Just as Joshua before him said, "But as for me and my house, we will serve the LORD," so David chose to worship, and not just sometimes—"at all times!"

Writer and preacher Charles Spurgeon said of David and his choice to praise:

> At all times and in every situation, under every circumstance, before, in and after trials, in bright days of glee, and dark nights of fear. He would never have done praising, never satisfied that he had done enough; always feeling that he had fell short of the

Lord's deservings. Happy is he whose fingers are wedded to his harp. He who praises God for mercies shall never want a mercy for which to praise. To bless the Lord is never unseasonable.[53]

David's praise was vocal and braggadocios, for he was confident in the One in whom he boasted! His God was omnipotent, omnipresent, and omniscient! David, like the apostle Paul, could assert:

> And I am convinced that nothing can ever separate us from God's love. Neither death nor life, neither angels nor demons, neither our fears for today nor our worries about tomorrow—not even the powers of hell can separate us from God's love (Romans 8:38 NLT).

David invited others to join in praise and worship in pursuit of the presence of God, "Oh, magnify the LORD with me, and let us exalt His name together" (Psalm 34:3). As the voices of His children rose together in adoration for our God and who He is, His heart must have swelled with joy.

Rev. A. W. Tozer wrote:

> Has it ever occurred to you that one hundred pianos all tuned to the same fork are automatically tuned to each other? They are of one accord by being tuned, not to each other, but to another standard to which each one must individually bow. So one hundred worshipers met together, each one looking away to Christ, are in heart nearer to each other than they

could possibly be, were they to become "unity" conscious and turn their eyes away from God to strive for closer fellowship.[54]

I believe God can't take His eyes of love off those who spend time in the passionate pursuit of Him. Every prayer catches His ear; every sigh touches His heart; every song of praise pleases Him. The crowd may pass by on the other side; your friends may forget you in the hustle of everyday life, but God *never* forgets! In verses 17 and 18 of Psalm 34, David writes:

> The righteous cry out, and the LORD hears, and delivers them out of all their troubles. The LORD is near to those who have a broken heart, and saves such as have a contrite spirit.

Pursuing God is one of the most rational, levelheaded, and fulfilling things a Believer can do. Set your heart today on pursuing God, and enjoy favor with Jehovah-Elyon—the Lord Most High!

—DISCUSSION—
MATERIAL

1. Read Psalm 23.

2. How was David's character molded as he watched his father's sheep?

3. Why did King Saul hate David?

4. How does jealousy affect the one who is jealous?

5. Have you ever found yourself in a pit of despair—distressed, in debt, and discontented—hoping against hope that someone would come along and point you in the right direction? What happened?

6. Where should our focus lie?

7. How do we develop a desire to pursue God?

8. Read Psalm 27:4. What was David's desire?

9. What does Psalm 34 teach us about pursuing God?

— SCRIPTURES ON —
PURSUING GOD

But if from thence thou shalt seek the LORD thy God, thou shalt find him, if thou seek him with all thy heart and with all thy soul.
DEUTERONOMY 4:29 KJV

I love them that love me; and those that seek me early shall find me.
PROVERBS 8:17 KJV

Then shall ye call upon me, and ye shall go and pray unto me, and I will hearken unto you.
JEREMIAH 29:12 KJV

Seek ye the LORD while he may be found, call ye upon him while he is near.
ISAIAH 55:6 KJV

The LORD is good unto them that wait for him, to the soul that seeketh him.
LAMENTATIONS 3:25 KJV

Ask, and it shall be given you; seek, and ye shall find; knock, and it shall be opened unto you: for every one that asketh receiveth; and he that seeketh findeth; and to him that knocketh it shall be opened.
MATTHEW 7:7–8 KJV

Let all those that seek thee rejoice and be glad in thee: let such as love thy salvation say continually, the LORD LORD be magnified.
PSALM 40:16 KJV

O God, thou art my God; early will I seek thee: my soul thirsteth for thee, my flesh longeth for thee in a dry and thirsty land, where no water is.
PSALM 63:1 KJV

The young lions do lack, and suffer hunger: but they that seek the LORD shall not want any good thing.
PSALM 34:10 KJV

And thou, Solomon my son, know thou the God of thy father, and serve him with a perfect heart and with a willing mind: for the LORD searcheth all hearts, and understandeth all the imaginations of the thoughts: if thou seek him, he will be found of thee; but if thou forsake him, he will cast thee off for ever.
1 CHRONICLES 28:9 KJV

With my whole heart have I sought thee: O let me not wander from thy commandments.
PSALM 119:10 KJV

Blessed are they that keep his testimonies, and that seek him with the whole heart.
PSALM 119:2 KJV

And they that know thy name will put their trust in thee: for thou, LORD, hast not forsaken them that seek thee.
PSALM 9:10 KJV

But seek ye first the kingdom of God, and his righteousness; and all these things shall be added unto you.
MATTHEW 6:33 KJV

I would seek unto God, and unto God would I commit my cause.
JOB 5:8 KJV

Seek the LORD and his strength, seek his face continually.
1 CHRONICLES 16:11 KJV

CHAPTER FOURTEEN

GOD IS ON HIS THRONE

The Lord reigns, He is clothed with majesty; the Lord is clothed, He has girded Himself with strength. Surely the world is established, so that it cannot be moved. Your throne is established from of old; You are from everlasting.

PSALM 93:1-2

ON OCTOBER 30, 1991, I WAS IN MADRID for the Middle East Peace Conference held following the First Gulf War. I had been told that Soviet President Mikhail Gorbachev and Israeli Prime Minister Yitzhak Shamir were to meet at the Russian Embassy. I quickly hired a taxi to rush me to the embassy building. The cab driver pulled up before the edifice, which was surrounded by a twelve-foot-high black wrought iron fence. When I climbed out of the vehicle, I immediately felt the chill of the rain and the 55-degree weather. After paying the taxi driver I walked over to the gate and asked, "Who is in charge here?" A Russian guard approached and growled, "I am in charge."

I demanded, "Open this gate and let me in."

Looking at me shivering in my overcoat, he snapped, "You have no credentials."

He was right; I had no official credentials to be a delegate to the Middle East Peace Conference, much less to demand entry to the embassy. I was not an ambassador to any nation; I had no official invitation. It was an impossible situation, but God is still on the throne and still in the miracle business. The only authority I had was in God's directive, "Go to Madrid, Spain." Not only had God sent me, He had infused me with faith for the impossible. I instinctively lifted my Bible and stated, "Here are my credentials."

The Russian looked at my Bible, grunted, stuck his nose in the air, and walked away.

"Come back here!" I insisted.

When he turned his head toward me I shook my finger authoritatively at him through the wrought iron barrier and declared, "In the name of Jesus, open this gate!" It was as if he had become a robot. The Russian instantly obeyed the command. Although still hostile, he pushed the button that opened the gate and allowed me to enter the Russian Embassy.

Soon, because of the power of God and His Word, I was ushered into the very room in which Mikhail Gorbachev and Yitzhak Shamir were to meet. It would be the first time in history the head of the Soviet Union and the prime minister of Israel would speak face-to-face.

As I left another of the meetings at the conference, the Syrian foreign minister stopped me. He pulled a picture of Yitzhak Shamir from his pocket and told me he intended to accuse the prime minister of being a terrorist, while he was a member of the *Irgun* (an early Israeli paramilitary organization). I borrowed a cell phone and called Benjamin Netanyahu to relate to him what I had been told. The next morning before the beginning of Shabbat and in the presence of President George H. W. Bush, President Gorbachev, and other world leaders, Mr. Shamir stood and said, "I have to leave now. I am an Orthodox Jew, and I leave these proceedings to my able delegation." Thirty minutes after he departed, the Syrian foreign minister stood to speak but faced only an empty chair where Shamir had sat. I was an observer, because God was and is on the throne of my life.

Who is on the throne of your life? Many Believers would automatically reply, "God." But is that really true? Men of integrity and honor, who dare to speak out against sin, become targets for egotistical men who place themselves above the will and call of God. In his book *The Kingdom of Self,* Earl Jabay, a clinically trained chaplain, wrote:

> The Kingdom of Self, understand, is in our heads. We spend years building this fantasy kingdom unto our own glory. The king's thinking becomes grandiose and his feelings ultimate. He believes all things can and must be done according to his will. And another thing; the king is never wrong. He is always right. Just ask him. He'll tell you.[55]

Is your heart a place devoted only to God, or has He been crowded out by other things of this world? Too often we begin our walk with Him filled with good intentions; we petition God wholeheartedly to occupy first place in our lives, but eventually the world begins to intrude. Our focus shifts to jobs, friends, even our family. These are all essential parts of life, but just remember that Jesus said, "But seek first the kingdom of God and His righteousness, and all these things shall be added to you" (see Matthew 6:33). If our priorities are in order, our motivation will be about pleasing God, putting Him first and foremost in our lives, and then He will add His blessings to our lives.

In Isaiah 6, the prophet was facedown in the Temple. He was exhausted from interceding for the children of Israel, and as his supplications filled the Temple, Jehovah responded with a vision for the prophet's eyes only. Isaiah was transported from the earthly Temple into the very throne room of God. There, his attention was not captured by the beauty of his surroundings, but was centered on the One whose Presence was overwhelming. God was reassuring Isaiah that He, Judah's Supreme King, was on the throne for all time and eternity. Isaiah described God's appearance:

> In the year that King Uzziah died, I saw the Lord, high and exalted, seated on a throne; and the train of his robe filled the temple. Above him were seraphim, each with six wings: With two wings they covered their faces, with two they covered their feet, and with two they were flying. And they were calling to one another: "Holy, holy, holy is the LORD Almighty; the whole earth is full of His glory." At the sound of their voices the doorposts and thresholds shook and the temple was filled with smoke (Isaiah 6:1–4 NIV).

No matter who sits on the thrones of earthly leadership, whether king, president, or prime minister, God is ultimately in control. No one ascends to office or holds it without God having allowed them to be placed there. Psalm 75:6–7 tells us:

For exaltation comes neither from the east nor from the west nor from the south. But God is the Judge: He puts down one, and exalts another.

Daniel reminds us in chapter 2:20–21:

Blessed be the name of God forever and ever, for wisdom and might are His. And He changes the times and the seasons; He removes kings and raises up kings; He gives wisdom to the wise and knowledge to those who have understanding.

And Solomon wrote in Proverbs 21:1:

The king's heart is in the hand of the LORD, like the rivers of water; He turns it wherever He wishes.

Isaiah's vision reminds me a little of standing before a magistrate in a courtroom. Dressed in black robes, he or she sits elevated above the others in the court. The judge is in charge, and holds the gavel that can dispatch anyone with a single strike. Like Isaiah, we stand in awe of earthly authority; how much more should we stand in awe of the God of the universe!

Isaiah suddenly found himself in a smoke-filled, heavenly temple. He was surrounded by the seraphim or "burning ones" of heaven who, though angelic beings, did not fail to cover themselves in the presence of Almighty God.

Second only to God's magnificence is His holiness—His unparalleled purity. Even as Isaiah was mesmerized in chapter 6 by the presence of God, he could hear a sound that could be identified with a chorus of angelic beings:

> And one cried to another and said: "Holy, holy, holy is the LORD of hosts; the whole earth is full of His glory!" And the posts of the door were shaken by the voice of him who cried out, and the house was filled with smoke.

Isaiah had entered into the presence of God and would come away with a renewed conviction of the holiness of God. It cannot be trivialized or marginalized. God is holy! He is so much more superior and resplendent than anything man can imagine. No earthly king can match His grandeur or His majesty. His very presence demands worship, devotion, and wonder.

God is love! God is holy! God is righteous! That doesn't mean that God meets the standard for those qualities; God *is* the standard by which all else is measured. Isaiah had entered into the presence of the epitome of holiness—Jehovah God. It is the character of the great I AM! Isaiah's response in verse 5 was immediate:

> Woe is me, for I am undone! Because I am a man of unclean lips, and I dwell in the midst of a people of unclean lips; for my eyes have seen the King, the LORD of hosts.

At the time of Isaiah's vision, Israel was at a crossroads—the people were economically prosperous but spiritually bankrupt. As one writer noted, Isaiah dwelled in the midst of "fat and happy sinners."[56]

The prophet, in the presence of pure holiness, realized his unworthiness. He had been concerned with the sinfulness of Judah; now he was concerned with his own impurity when seen under the microscope of God's purity. Isaiah realized he had no place to hide—he was doomed. As he lay prostrate before the Lord God Almighty, he cried that he was a man of unclean lips and he dwelled in the midst of a people whose lips were unclean. Jehovah, however, did not abandon Isaiah to his woeful status, for He is the God of redemption:

> Then one of the seraphim flew to me with a live coal in his hand, which he had taken with tongs from the altar. With it he touched my mouth and said, "See, this has touched your lips; your guilt is taken away and your sin atoned for (Isaiah 6:6–7 NIV).

What is our reaction when we realize the holiness of God? Do we truly grasp its meaning? Do we dishonor God to the point that He simply becomes our pal rather than the holy and righteous God? A true encounter with God always brings inevitable change. Either your commitment to Him grows deeper, or you harden your heart and perish spiritually. Psalm 93:2 reminds us that God's throne is everlasting—it always has been and forever will be.

In Lamentations 5:19, Jeremiah cried, "You, O LORD, remain forever; Your throne from generation to generation." What better assurance could we have than to know that God is on His throne and beside Him sits the "Lamb slain from the foundation of the world" (see Revelation 13:8). It is a position of absolute power and command. Nothing surprises God; He knows before a thought makes its way into our consciousness what we are going to do. He knows the answer even before we know the question. He is aware of the solution even before we encounter a problem! Because He occupies the throne on high and can see the end from the beginning. According to theologian Arthur W. Pink:

> Divine sovereignty means that God is God in fact, as well as in name, that He is on the Throne of the universe, directing all things, working all things "after the counsel of His own will" (Eph. 1:11).[57]

Daily events portend change, yet God never changes. He is faithful and immovable. Songsmith Dottie Rambo wrote the spiritual "I Go to the Rock." The chorus reminds us:

> The earth all around me is sinking sand
> But on Jesus the solid Rock I stand
> When I need a shelter
> When I need a friend
> I go to the Rock[58]

Perhaps the writer of Hebrews said it best and most succinctly in chapter 13, verse 8:

> Jesus Christ is the same yesterday, today, and forever.

Have you heard the old saying, "When the going gets tough; the tough get going"? The reality is: "When the going gets tough, go to Jesus!" It is a move you will never regret; for it is there that you will find the help you need. It is in His presence that you will find favor with Him.

Hebrews 4:16 reminds us that as Believers, because of our

relationship with Christ, we can "come boldly to the throne of grace, that we may obtain mercy and find grace to help in time of need."

There are those who place great value in who they know—especially if those persons are considered to be the movers and shakers of the world. Those "in the know" will quickly recite a litany of who's who and what's what in order to impress others. But you and I are intimately acquainted with the only One who really matters—God the Father. We are heirs of God and joint heirs with Jesus Christ, and are sealed by the Holy Spirit (see Ephesians 1:13-14). Because we have a close, personal relationship with the triune Godhead, we have the privilege of entering the throne room anytime we choose. Revelation 5:8 says that the prayers of the saints are "golden bowls full of incense."

Unlike those who may spend great sums of money to hobnob with the "A-listers," our entrée is a gift freely given, and yet it cost Jesus everything. God's grace has made it possible for us to have continual access to the throne and He who sits upon it.

In 1 John 5:14-15, the apostle wrote these words of encouragement to the followers of Christ:

> Now this is the confidence that we have in Him, that if we ask anything according to His will, He hears us. And if we know that He hears us, whatever we ask, we know that we have the petitions that we have asked of Him.

As obedient children, we know that we can approach His throne with the assurance that if we ask according to His will, Jehovah will hear and respond. That, my friend, is the most important relationship you and I can have—one of fellowship and favor *with* God.

—DISCUSSION—
MATERIAL

1. Read Isaiah 6.

2. Have you ever been in the presence of someone the world considers important?

3. What was your reaction?

4. How would you feel if you came face-to-face with Jesus?

5. How do you think you would react?

6. What was Isaiah's response?

7. What is the most important relationship we can have?

8. Read Hebrews 4:15. What is one of the greatest benefits of being a Believer?

— SCRIPTURES ON —
GOD'S THRONE

Your throne, O God, is forever and ever; a scepter of righteousness is the scepter of Your kingdom.
PSALM 45:6

The LORD is in His holy temple, the LORD's throne is in heaven;
PSALM 11:4

God reigns over the nations; God sits on His holy throne.
PSALM 47:8

Righteousness and justice are the foundation of Your throne; mercy and truth go before Your face.
PSALM 89:14

Your throne is established from of old; You are from everlasting.
PSALM 93:2

Heaven is My throne, and earth is My footstool.
ISAIAH 66:1

So Jesus said to them, "Assuredly I say to you, that in the regeneration, when the Son of Man sits on the throne of His glory, you who have followed Me will also sit on twelve thrones, judging the twelve tribes of Israel.
MATTHEW 19:28

But to the Son He says: *"Your throne, O God, is forever and ever; a scepter of righteousness is the scepter of Your kingdom.*
HEBREWS 1:8

Looking unto Jesus, the author and finisher of our faith, who for the joy that was set before Him endured the cross, despising the shame, and has sat down at the right hand of the throne of God.

HEBREWS 12:2

Therefore they are before the throne of God, and serve Him day and night in His temple. And He who sits on the throne will dwell among them. They shall neither hunger anymore nor thirst anymore; the sun shall not strike them, nor any heat; for the Lamb who is in the midst of the throne will shepherd them and lead them to living fountains of waters. And God will wipe away every tear from their eyes.

REVELATION 7:15–17

EPILOGUE

And he showed me a pure river of water of life, clear as crystal, proceeding from the throne of God and of the Lamb.

REVELATION 22:1

THE STORY OF TWELVE-YEAR-OLD JESUS staying behind in Jerusalem is one with which most of us are familiar. It is, however, verse 52 that garners the most attention for no other reason than that a true Believer wants to know how to grow in favor with God and man. We read in Luke 2:41–52:

> His parents went to Jerusalem every year at the Feast of the Passover. And when He was twelve years old, they went up to Jerusalem according to the custom of the feast. When they had finished the days, as they returned, the Boy Jesus lingered behind in Jerusalem. And Joseph and His mother did not know it; but supposing Him to have been in the company, they went a day's journey, and sought Him among their relatives and acquaintances. So when they did not find Him, they returned to Jerusalem, seeking Him. Now so it was that after three days they found

Him in the temple, sitting in the midst of the teachers, both listening to them and asking them questions. And all who heard Him were astonished at His understanding and answers. So when they saw Him, they were amazed; and His mother said to Him, "Son, why have You done this to us? Look, Your father and I have sought You anxiously." And He said to them, "Why did you seek Me? Did you not know that I must be about My Father's business?" But they did not understand the statement which He spoke to them. Then He went down with them and came to Nazareth, and was subject to them, but His mother kept all these things in her heart. And Jesus increased in wisdom and stature, and in favor with God and men.

Sadly, this is the only story in the Bible of Jesus as a child in His formative years. In fact, the next time we encounter Jesus in Scripture, it is in Luke 3 when Jesus had gone down to the Jordan to be baptized by John. As He arose from the water, verses 21–22 tell us:

When all the people were baptized, it came to pass that Jesus also was baptized; and while He prayed, the heaven was opened. And the Holy Spirit descended in bodily form like a dove upon Him, and a voice came from heaven which said, "You are My beloved Son; in You I am well pleased."

We can only determine from those verses that Jesus' life had found favor with God. God loved the man, Jesus, and grace was multiplied to Him daily. His heavenly Father delighted in Him.

What did Jesus do that was so unusual? He simply lived His life to please the Father. He worked at and completed whatever task Joseph assigned Him. He attended school in the synagogue where the Torah was studied daily. Jesus, the one who had given the writer of Psalm 119 the scripture, "Your word I have hidden in my heart, that I might not sin against You," fed upon that passage to fortify His own spirit. He was obedient to his mother's bidding even as he played with the other children in the village of Nazareth. Perhaps He read Solomon's words in Proverbs 3:1–4 (NIV):

> My son, do not forget my teaching, but keep my commands in your heart, for they will prolong your life many years and bring you peace and prosperity. Let love and faithfulness never leave you; bind them around your neck, write them on the tablet of your heart. Then you will win favor and a good name in the sight of God and man.

It was in the ordinary, everyday things that Jesus learned the lesson He taught in Matthew 25:21—that if we are faithful over a few things, we will someday rule over many things.

We find favor with God when we are faithful in the small things. Too often we eschew grace and try to earn favor with God by doing something monumental, earth-shattering, or bigger than life. Just as Jesus went about doing the will of the Father daily, so should we.

Pastor Loren Covarrubias wrote of the child, Jesus:

> You are not ready to be a king unless you've learned what it means to be a servant. Jesus Himself was subject to the law of His parents. This was the proving

ground making Him ready for His ministry as the Son of God.[59]

We can rest in the truth that God loves us, and the proof of that love and favor is present in the Person of Jesus Christ. Thomas à Kempis wrote:

Without the Way, there is no going,
Without the Truth, there is no knowing,
Without the Life, there is no living.[60]

God is our Father, and we are His beloved children. Ephesians 1:3–6 tells us:

Blessed be the God and Father of our Lord Jesus Christ, who has blessed us with every spiritual blessing in the heavenly places in Christ, just as He chose us in Him before the foundation of the world, that we should be holy and without blame before Him in love, having predestined us to adoption as sons by Jesus Christ to Himself, according to the good pleasure of His will, to the praise of the glory of His grace, by which He made us *accepted in the Beloved* (emphasis mine).

Because of that acceptance, we have favor with God and are free to enjoy His peace, protection, blessings, deliverance, grace, forgiveness, and love. Isaiah 41:10 in the Amplified version of the Bible assures us:

Fear not [there is nothing to fear], for I am with you; do not look around you in terror and be dismayed, for I am your God. I will strengthen and harden you to difficulties, yes, I will help you; yes, I will hold you up and retain you with My [victorious] right hand of rightness and justice.

Why would God assure us that we are to "fear not" if we live in His favor? It is because our Father knows that we will be faced with challenges and difficulties that will try our faith but not rob us of our favor with Him.

Even through the trials that will surely come our way, God adds benefits daily that help us turn those adversities into victories.

Can you hear the Father and His angels leaning over the balcony of heaven shouting encouragement, urging you onward, reminding you that it *is* Who you know and Whose you are? My friend, don't hesitate to pray for favor—for yourself, your spouse, your children and grandchildren. Then, as Jesus did, walk before the Father in integrity, in obedience, and in faith. Paul reminds us in 2 Corinthians 6:2 (NIV) of God's Word to His children: "In the time of my favor I heard you, and in the day of salvation I helped you."

—SCRIPTURES ON—
FAVOR WITH GOD

For thou, LORD, wilt bless the righteous; with favour wilt thou compass him as with a shield.
PSALM 5:12 KJV

Thou shalt arise, and have mercy upon Zion: for the time to favour her, yea, the set time, is come.
PSALM 102:13 KJV

And said, My LORD, if now I have found favour in thy sight, pass not away, I pray thee, from thy servant.
GENESIS 18:3 KJV

For his anger endureth but a moment; in his favour is life: weeping may endure for a night, but joy cometh in the morning.
PSALM 30:5 KJV

And Jesus increased in wisdom and stature, and in favour with God and man.
LUKE 2:52 KJV

For thou art the glory of their strength: and in thy favour our horn shall be exalted.
PSALM 89:17 KJV

Now God had brought Daniel into favour and tender love with the prince of the eunuchs.
DANIEL 1:9 KJV

In the light of the king's countenance is life; and his favour is as a cloud of the latter rain.
PROVERBS 16:15 KJV

Remember me, O LORD, with the favour that thou bearest unto thy people: O visit me with thy salvation.
PSALM 106:4 KJV

(ENDNOTES)

1. http://biblehub.com/matthew/14-25.htm; accessed July 2014.

2. http://www.prayers-for-special-help.com/footprints-prayer.html#sthash.rtvT7lvK.dpuf; accessed July 2014.

3. http://www.metrolyrics.com/his-eye-is-on-the-sparrow-lyrics-lauryn-hill.html; accessed July 2014.

4. Hudson Taylor Quotes: http://christian-quotes.ochristian.com/; accessed September 2012.

5. Originally from *Our Daily Bread*, the original concept for this story is found online at: http://www.christianglobe.com/Illustrations/theDetails.asp?whichOne=p&whichFile=protection.

6. See Psalm 1:1

7. Psalm 91, http://www.biblestudytools.com/commentaries/treasury-of-david/psalms-91-1.html; accessed July 2014.

8. http://defendchristianfaith.blogspot.com/2010/10/inspiring-story-gods-protection.html; accessed August 2014.

9. http://biblegodquotes.com/sometimes-god-calms-the-storm/; accessed August 2014.

10. Charles Spurgeon, "A View of God's Glory," The Spurgeon Archive, http://www.spurgeon.org/sermons/3120.htm; accessed July 2014.

11. Charles R. Swindoll, *Simple Faith* (Nashville, TN: W Group, a division of Thomas Nelson, Inc., 2003), 23.

12. John MacArthur, *The Beatitudes, The Only Way to Happiness* (Chicago, IL: Moody Press, 1998), 34–35.

13. http://www.lyrics.com/if-jesus-came-to-your-house-lyrics-red-sovine.html; accessed July 2014.

14. G. Campbell Morgan, "The Gospel According to Matthew," Chapter Nine, Copyright 1929, http://www.baptistbiblebelievers.com/LinkClick.aspx?fileticket=voDoiuSWN3I%3d&tabid=322&mid=1057; accessed August 2014.

15. Jim Cymbala, *The Life God Blesses* (Chicago, IL: Moody Press, 1998), 11.

16. Pastor Ed Rea, http://packinghouseredlands.org/devotional/?p=4428; accessed August 2014.

17. Dr. Neil Chadwick, former pastor, Crossroads Assembly of God Church, Hamburg, NJ, http://www.joyfulministry.org/godsjoyt.htm; accessed August 2014.

18. John Piper: "The Pleasure of God in the Good of His People" http://www.desiringgod.org/sermons/the-pleasure-of-god-in-the-good-of-his-people; accessed August 2014.

19. Dr. Steve Rodeheaver, Exodus 4:18–31, "God Seeks Moses' Life," http://www.crivoice.org/biblestudy/exodus/bbex7.html; accessed September 2014.

20. C. F. Keil and Franz Delitzsch: *Commentary on the Old Testament, vol. 2* (Peabody, MA: Hendrickson Publishers, 2006), 34.

21. Dietrich Bonhoeffer, http://www.christianitytoday.com/ch/131christians/martyrs/bonhoeffer.html; accessed August 2014.

22. J. I. Packer, *Knowing God* (Downers Grove, IL: InterVarsity Press, 1973), 226, https://www.goodreads.com/quotes/312397-in-the-new-testament-grace-means-god-s-love-in-action; accessed November 2014.

23. Rev. John Sowers, "The Woman Caught in Adultry," November 25, 2012, http://www.spokanefpc.org/images/uploads/attachments/121125-transcript-of-sermon.pdf; accessed August 2014.

24. Rev. Robert L. (Bob)Deffinbaugh, https://bible.org/seriespage/grace-god-part-i-ephesians-15-12-21-10; accessed August 2014.

25. "http://www.spurgeon.us/mind_and_heart/quotes/g2.htm; accessed August 2014.

26. Max Lucado, *The Gift for all People, Thoughts on God's Great Grace* (Sisters, OR: Multnomah Publishers, 1999), 132.

27. Max Lucado, 88.

28. Charles Swindoll, *The Grace Awakening* (Dallas, TX: Word Publishing, 1990), 114.

29. Martin Luther, http://www.christianquote.com/newquote/quotesview.php?id=183; accessed September 2014.

30. C. S. Lewis, *The Problem of Pain*, https://www.biblegateway.com/devotionals/cs-lewis-daily/2014/06/19; accessed August 2014.

31. David G. Meyers, *The Pursuit of Happiness: Discovering the Pathway to Fulfillment, Well-Being, and Enduring Personal Joy* (New York: Avon Books, Inc., 1992), 178.

32. Rick Warren, *The Purpose Driven Life* (Grand Rapids, MI: Zondervan, 2002), 66–67.

33. http://www.usmb.org/news/article/Psalm-95-What-is-worship.html; accessed August 2014.

34. Rev. A. W. Tozer, "God Enjoys His Creation," http://www.cmalliance.org/devotions/tozer?id=1417; accessed September 2014.

35. Oswald Chambers, *My Utmost for His Highest*, "The Forgiveness of God," http://utmost.org/the-forgiveness-of-god/; accessed September 2014.

36. "A Story of a 92 Years Old Pastor," http://achristianpilgrim.wordpress.com/2010/09/17/jesus-loves-me-this-i-know-for-the-bible-tells-me-so/; accessed September 2014.

37. C. S. Lewis, *The Four Loves* (New York: Harcourt Brace, 1960), quoted by http://hillshepherd.blogspot.com/2010/02/cs-lewis.html; accessed September 2014.

38. Ellis J. Crum, "He Paid a Debt He Did Not Owe," http://www.touchjesussongs.net/lyricspage15.html; Accessed September 2014.

39. "God Is Love," http://www.uccb.org/sermons/2009/20090510/1John4GodIsLove.htm#_ftn1; accessed September 2014.

40. Francis A. Schaeffer, *The Mark of the Christian* (Downers Grove, IL: InterVarsity Press), 25, 35.

41. http://www.cyberhymnal.org/htm/o/l/oltwnlmg.htm; accessed August 2014.

42. Dr. Charles Stanley, "How Can I Have God's Peace?" http://www.intouch.org/you/article-archive/content?topic=how_can_i_have_god_s_peace_article#.VBH_To10w2k; accessed September 2014.

43. Bertha Spafford Vester, *Our Jerusalem: An American Family in the Holy City 1881–1949* (Jerusalem: Ariel Publishing House, 1988), 34.

44. Ibid, p. 38.

45. Public Domain; words by Horatio Spafford, score by Phillip P. Bliss, 1873; http://www.cyberhymnal.org/htm/i/t/i/itiswell.htm. Note: Phillip Bliss died in a train accident shortly after completing the score.

46. David Wilkerson, http://sermons.worldchallenge.org/node/1035; accessed July 2014.

47. http://en.wikipedia.org/wiki/Mission:_Impossible; accessed August 2014.

48. Elisabeth Elliott, *A Chance to Die: The Life and Legacy of Amy Carmichael*, quoted at http://www.goodreads.com/work/quotes/121523-a-chance-to-die-the-life-and-legacy-of-amy-carmichael; accessed August 2014.

49. Michelle Wallace, "When You Pray," *Living Magazine*, August 2014, p. 53.

50. "Footprints in the Sand," http://www.prayers-for-special-help.com/footprints-prayer.html#sthash.Qfrg35EA.dpuf; accessed August 2014.

51. Tommy Tenney, *God Chasers: My Soul Follows Hard After Thee* (Shippensburg, PA: Destiny Image Publishers, Inc., 2001), back cover copy.

52. Ibid.

53. Charles Haddon Spurgeon, https://www.facebook.com/Charles.Haddon.Spurgeon; accessed September 2014.

54. A. W. Tozer, *The Pursuit of God* quotes, http://www.goodreads.com/work/quotes/203894-pursuit-of-god; accessed September 2014.

55. Earl Jabay, *The Kingdom of Self*, Logos International, 1980; as quoted on http://jollyblogger.typepad.com/jollyblogger/2008/07/what-if-its-jus.html; accessed August 2014.

56. Johnold Strey, "Three Lessons About the Triune God," http://pastorstrey.wordpress.com/2009/06/08/sermon-on-isaiah-6/; accessed August 2014.

57. A. W. Pink, "The Attributes of God," http://www.pbministries.org/books/pink/Attributes/attrib_06.htm; accessed August 2014.

58. Dottie Rambo, "I Go to the Rock," http://www.southern-gospel-music-lyrics.com/dottie-rambo-i-go-to-the-rock.html; accessed August 2014.

59. Loren Covarrubias, *Discovering Favor with God* (Shippensburg, PA: Destiny Image, 2004), 28.

60. Thomas à Kempis, http://izquotes.com/quote/243132/.

MICHAEL DAVID EVANS, the #1 *New York Times* bestselling author, is an award-winning journalist/Middle East analyst. Dr. Evans has appeared on hundreds of network television and radio shows including *Good Morning America, Crossfire* and *Nightline*, and *The Rush Limbaugh Show*, and on Fox Network, *CNN World News*, NBC, ABC, and CBS. His articles have been published in the *Wall Street Journal, USA Today, Washington Times, Jerusalem Post* and newspapers worldwide. More than twenty-five million copies of his books are in print, and he is the award-winning producer of nine documentaries based on his books.

Dr. Evans is considered one of the world's leading experts on Israel and the Middle East, and is one of the most sought-after speakers on that subject. He is the chairman of the board of the Ten Boom Holocaust Museum in Haarlem, Holland, and is the founder of Israel's first Christian museum—Friends of Zion: Heroes and History—in Jerusalem.

Dr. Evans has authored a number of books including: *History of Christian Zionism, Showdown with Nuclear Iran, Atomic Iran, The Next Move Beyond Iraq, The Final Move Beyond Iraq*, and *Countdown*. His body of work also includes the novels *Seven Days, GameChanger, The Samson Option, The Four Horsemen, The Locket, Born Again: 1967*, and his most recent, *The Columbus Code*.

✦ ✦ ✦

Michael David Evans is available to speak or for interviews.
Contact: EVENTS@drmichaeldevans.com.

BOOKS BY: MIKE EVANS

TO PURCHASE, CONTACT: orders@timeworthybooks.com
P. O. BOX 30000, PHOENIX, AZ 85046